Don't let the title confuse you. *Total Financial Awakening* is a masterclass not only in financial freedom but also in the freedom to live the life you want. Andrey Sokurec paints a clear picture of what is possible if you are ready to embrace the Four Freedoms.
—Harvey Mackay, author of the #1 New York Times bestseller, *Swim with the Sharks Without Being Eaten Alive*

Total Financial Awakening helps you see the importance of taking responsibility for your life. As you read between the pages, the process of how to start in the real estate business is explained with simple and easy, yet profound, concepts that will help you be in control of your own destiny.
—Jack Canfield, co-author of the New York Times bestselling *Chicken Soup for the Soul®* series, America's #1 Success Coach, and author of *The Success Principles™*

In his book, *Total Financial Awakening*, Andrey Sokurec demonstrates how using strategic thinking and my 80% Approach Method as a great pathway, leading you toward freedom of time, the best relationships, higher purpose, and financial success.
—Dan Sullivan, Founder & President of The Strategic Coach®, Inc.

Total Financial Awakening will give you a great motivation to change the way you think about your money and how you can use real estate (or rent estate as I do) as a tool to become financially free.

—Kevin Ortner, President & CEO
of Renters Warehouse

This book will make you believe that you, too, can be financially free. When applying the principles within, you can claim your life back and spend time doing what you love to do, including what most want and desire … spending quality time with your family and kids.

—Jonathan Passley,
Marketing Expert & Consultant

I started reading *Total Financial Awakening* on the train into work this morning, and I almost missed my stop because I was getting into the story and wanted to truly read it to the end—and see how both Roger and Susan were able to change their lives because of figuring out their Four Freedoms, using Dan Sullivan's The Strategic Coach® approach. Amazing.

—Serafina Puilo, Director of Legal Services
for The Strategic Coach, Inc.

TOTAL FINANCIAL AWAKENING

ESCAPE THE GRIND, DISCOVER FREEDOM, AND RECLAIM YOUR LIFE THROUGH REAL ESTATE INVESTING

A Business Fable

TOTAL FINANCIAL AWAKENING

ESCAPE THE GRIND, DISCOVER FREEDOM, AND RECLAIM YOUR LIFE THROUGH REAL ESTATE INVESTING

A Business Fable

ANDREY SOKUREC
WITH
ALEX DELENDIK

AUTHOR ACADEMY elite

Printed in the United States of America

Published by Author Academy Elite
PO Box 43, Powell, OH 43065
www.AuthorAcademyElite.com

Identifiers:
LCCN: 2020908187
ISBN: 978-1-64746-260-4 (paperback)
ISBN: 978-1-64746-261-1 (hardback)
ISBN: 978-1-64746-262-8 (ebook)

Available in paperback, hardback, and e-book

Cover design by Debbie O'Byrne.

AndreySokurec.com
HomesteadRoad.com

*for those
who have nothing
except the
burning desire
to succeed*

TABLE OF CONTENTS

ACKNOWLEDGMENTS

~ Andrey Sokurec & Alex Delendik

First of all, I would like to give thanks to my wife and family, who put up with far too many long hours when getting this business successfully off the ground.

I would also like to acknowledge my parents for supporting me in anything and everything I wanted to do and try. I deeply appreciate you, Mom and Dad.

To my business partner and chief operations officer, Alex Delendik, for whom I could not do without.

Our 40 employees, who have the same vision as I—to provide a feeling of joy and experience when people want to sell the house easy and stress free without doing a lot of repairs.

And to my many mentors, who I either personally studied under or ravishingly read their books, following their directions to the letter: Roberto Rodriguez, Jack Canfield, Harvey Mackay, Robert Kiyosaki, Dan Sullivan, Michael E. Gerber, just to name a few.

To Roberto Rodriguez, the best friend who helped me to close my first deal.

Not necessarily the last person to acknowledge, by any means, is you, Dear Reader. For it is the desire, the fire in your belly you have to create the best life for you and your family. This is the reason … *you* are the reason I wrote this book.

My deepest gratitude and thanks to you all for pushing me to do and be the best.

If it weren't for the people listed above and for the hundreds that are not, I would not be where I am today. I know that sounds cliché, but I can tell you, as Roger Alcott put his faith in his wife, kids, and mentors, I placed my fears aside and followed a plan to my ***Total Financial Awakening***.

AUTHORS' NOTE

Life has a great deal up its sleeve.

—Joseph Brodsky

Over the course of the last few months, as I've been working on this book, friends and associates have marveled at why I would create a fictional account of a man and his family as he changed his entire life to create a new reality for himself.

Some have even said that my own story would be better and more inspiring—after all, I immigrated from Belarus in 2004 as a young man with no money and no credit, yet here I am, fifteen years later, with a multi-million-dollar real estate business that buys, sells, and rents homes, much like my protagonist, Roger Alcott.

The truth is, just like Roger and just like you, I had to make a decision.

For me, it came down to knowing that the United States offered the greatest opportunity for the financial freedom I longed for. In my early days here, of course, I was hampered by my language skills, but in the evenings, after I left the construction jobs where I was working as a laborer, I would go to my local library and read or listen to the audio files of works like Jack Canfield's *How to Double Your Income*, Napoleon Hill's *Think and Grow Rich*, and, of course, Robert Kiyosaki's *Cashflow Quadrant*.

Through these and many more, I learned that real estate offered the perfect opportunity for me.

Just like it does for you, Dear Reader.

There are certainly autobiographical parts in the journey of my character of Roger Alcott, and he certainly is in a far better financial situation than I was when I started out, but the reality is this—anyone, if they choose, can become successful in real estate. It takes hard work, it takes determination, and it takes time, but the end result—the financial freedom, the ability to take off for a day, or a week, or a month— more than makes up for the hard work one must put in at the beginning.

I wish you success in your journey, and I applaud you for taking this first step by reading my book.

Andrey Sokurec
Alex Delendik

CHAPTER ONE

A man should never neglect his family for business.

—Walt Disney

Spring came early to Atlanta, and even though the dogwoods and azaleas were in full bloom, the telltale signs of spring in the Deep South would be gone before Easter this year. Little League baseball practice had started, and the first whispers of success for the Braves were being announced on sports talk radio all over Atlanta.

"The one bright spot for sports in Atlanta," mused Roger Alcott, looking out of his office window in Vinings toward the view of the Atlanta skyline to the south.

Both of his sons played sports. His wife, Susan, chauffeured Brent and Chris around to sports and after-school functions throughout the year. As a younger man, Roger had played Division Two football at his alma mater, Furman, but couldn't remember the last time he had made time to actually watch a game.

Looking up from the spreadsheets that populated his computer screen, he realized it was after 7:00 p.m., so he decided to take a short break and then wrap up work for the day in the next hour. Rooting through the breakroom refrigerator, he found a Diet Pepsi he vaguely remembered putting in there a few weeks ago and decided to claim it.

He popped the tab, leaned back against the counter, and mentally ticked through the tasks he still had to do for the night. "I've got to sort out this backhaul issue with St. Louis, go over the Smithfield account proposal, and then figure out what we're going to do with Jacksonville and the Port improvements. We've got to get more leverage in there ..." He let the sentence trickle off, speaking to no one in particular since the normal employees—the worker bees—always darted out of the Alliant Logistics offices at 5:00 p.m. like the building was on fire.

Roger didn't really hold a grudge against them; he knew they didn't make any kind of *real* money. They were largely responsible for doing the things that men like Roger—sales managers, vice presidents, and executives—told them to do. If you could leave promptly at five o'clock, that just meant your boss wasn't paying attention to all the things that needed to be done.

A noise in the hallway startled Roger back from his thoughts, and he peeked out of the breakroom to see Bradley *Somebody*, a new outside sales rep that Alliant had recently brought on board.

Bradley looked like he was guilty of something, but then Roger noticed the kid's tie was loosened, and the top button of his shirt was unbuttoned. Alliant Logistics had a very strict dress code for all salaried employees. Roger always thought it a little Draconian and certainly paid homage to Tom Watson and his ideas from IBM, but Bradley was obviously nervous that a senior executive had just spied him out of uniform.

"Uhh, Mr. Alcott? Hi. I don't know if you remember me ..." stammered the kid.

"Absolutely! Bradley Stevens, isn't it?" The name had swum up to the top of Roger's brain suddenly.

"Yes, sir! I didn't think you'd remember me. I've only been with Alliant for a month or so."

Roger smiled. "Well, Bradley, when I was a young outside sales guy, I figured out I'd better be able to remember every name of anyone that I met, because otherwise, they might not think I respected them. To tell the truth, I just learned how to do it to be a better closer. So, what are you still doing here this time of the evening, Bradley?"

"Well, ummm, I had some things I needed to get sorted out for my little office, you know, knick-knacks for my desk, some pictures of my folks, and a picture of my girlfriend. And I am trying to learn all the software so I can write deals better and faster. I'd ask you why you're still here, but everyone already told me. You're like a machine that never stops."

"Yeah, I guess I am. So, it would seem that at least a few of the people you've met are still calling me the *Terminator*?"

Bradley suddenly looked very nervous. Is it proper to discuss condescending nicknames with a superior in your company? Especially if those condescending nicknames were *about* the superior you were talking to?

With obvious discomfort, Bradley replied, "Ummm, gee. Well, yes, sir."

"Well, kid, I'll tell you what. I could tell you that I'm here because the west coast is still open for business, but the truth is, I've got a ton of work to do based on sorting out some new ventures and opportunities for Alliant. Besides, there's a ball game tonight."

"Mr. Alcott, I didn't think you were a baseball fan?"

Roger smiled. "No, my kids' team. They're playing tonight, so my wife has them all sorted out. That gives me an extra few hours here at the office."

"You don't go to your kids' games?" asked Bradley, looking puzzled.

"Oh, I've been to a few of them over the years, but the way I see it, a man has a bigger responsibility to his family. We've got to provide for them. We've got a beautiful home, my kids go to private school, and we can take great vacations. In return, though, I have to be here, grinding away. Sure, I hear some whining from Chris and Brent—I've got twins—but I know they'll realize when they're older that they could do all the stuff they wanted because I wasn't there at the house, like some underemployed loser waiting on them to get home from school."

Roger took another drink from his Diet Pepsi and continued, "You see, Bradley, it took me a few years to realize that in order for me to get ahead, I had to be willing to do the things other guys wouldn't. When they were closing down their computer at 4:30 p.m. on a Friday and goofing off until it was time to leave, I was still grinding.

"Six, seven, even eight o'clock at night. Saturday mornings, sitting in here checking on deliveries, stopping in Sunday mornings to check on my schedules for the next week. It's easier now with technology, but those actions I took? They were the reasons I've been successful.

"I out-worked the other guys. When the kids were born, I was able to slack off a little bit, but I was so used to working, I just kept on. In the end, that hard work allows me to provide a level of comfort for my family and myself that I couldn't if I wasn't busting my ass seventy or eighty hours a week."

He continued, "In the end, I guess I've just always figured that being able to give them the things they want is better than me sitting there on my duff watching a Little League game. Riding in their mother's Range Rover is a helluva lot cooler than sitting in some crummy minivan like all the other moms."

Bradley smiled and agreed, "Yes, sir. I hated when Mom would pick me up from school in her Grand Caravan. I guess you're right. Well, Mr. Alcott ..."

"Please, just call me Roger."

"Uh, yessir," said Bradley, obviously a little skeptical of this newfound freedom. "Well, Roger, sorry to have disturbed your break. I'd better get back and get finished up. I'm supposed to be meeting Elaine—that's my girlfriend—at the Buckhead Diner here in about forty-five minutes."

"Goodnight then, Bradley, enjoy your meal. Great restaurant. I've only got another hour or so too. I'll see you tomorrow."

Bradley Stevens returned to his office and looked around. He watched one last training video mindlessly—something about tips and tricks for booking out backhauls—and then stuffed his notes and manuals into his attaché case.

As he walked out of the office of Alliant Logistics, he chanced to look back to the third floor, the sales floor, and in the late evening light, he could vaguely make out the form of Roger Alcott pacing in his office, the only office with a light still on. Roger's body language suggested he was talking on the phone.

He got behind the wheel of his little Honda Civic and had to wonder about the conversation with Roger. *What drove a man to have a family that he hardly ever saw? Why claw and fight your way to the top of the heap with a company like Alliant only not to be the one who was enjoying the fruits of your own labor?*

"It really must suck to be Mr. Alcott," he said to the dashboard. And with that, he put the little Honda in gear and drove out to meet Elaine for dinner.

CHAPTER TWO

The faults of the burglar are the
qualities of the financier.

—George Bernard Shaw

Roger awoke with a start the next morning with the weird feeling that something was wrong. He mentally ticked off the usual worries—no potential Alliant problems, his wife and kids were home, and the security systems still flashed the "all clear" message on the keyboard on the wall of the master bedroom.

He looked at the clock, 6:34 a.m., and on a Saturday morning, his mental alarm clock would be going off in another twenty minutes.

So, what the hell had woken him up?

He listened and heard nothing in the house, but he could hear muffled voices outside and the faint sound of a powerful motor.

Shrugging into an old pair of pants and a t-shirt, Roger peeked out the window in the bathroom and could see two police officers walking through the neighbor's yard. The O'Bannions had moved out six months ago, and the house had been quietly languishing, empty and for sale since then. He quickly moved to his closet, slipped on an old pair of shoes, and stepped out the back door where he hailed the one officer he spied.

"Morning, officer. I'm Roger Alcott. What's going on?"

The cop, Roger could now see he was actually a deputy, turned to the sound of Roger's voice, obviously identified him as not being a threat, and walked over.

"Morning, sir. I'm guessing you're the owner of this home?" he asked, indicating Roger's house.

Roger nodded, and the deputy continued, "Neighborhood Watch saw the front door on your neighbor's house was open about 5:15 this morning. We got here about half an hour ago and are writing it up as a criminal mischief call. Doesn't look like there's anything in the house to take."

"Yes, sir," Roger said, "the O'Bannions lived there until about six months ago. Couple went through a nasty divorce, and the court ordered them to sell the house. I think the ex-wife stayed local, but the husband went back to Ohio or somewhere in the Midwest. They had more than a few nasty fights in the front yard about who was going to keep what, but I thought the house was empty."

"Got it," said the deputy, writing notes on a little pad of paper. "Did you guys hear anything this morning? Car? Car door? Anyone talking?"

"Nope, I slept like a baby. I fell asleep about two o'clock after checking on some deliveries my company was handling today, but I never heard anything."

Still writing, the young officer asked Roger, "So, do you know anything about the previous owners?"

"Fairly typical for the neighborhood. Steve made pretty good money, and his wife spent it just as easily. I really think he was married to his job more than he was married to Michelle, but I never heard anything bad about their marriage or their relationship."

Roger added, "Actually, I think Michelle just got fed up with Steve never being home. Lord knows her taste was expensive, and the man was constantly buying her things. I haven't been in the house in a couple of years, but it was always decorated perfectly and clean enough to eat off the floor. I guess they still haven't been able to sell it, but sooner or later, I'm sure they will."

The deputy, Roger could see his nametag now, Deputy *Jenkins,* thought for a minute and asked, "So, did the wife handle the cleaning? Did she have some-one to clean house? Maybe a housekeeper who might still have a key?"

He thought a second, shook his head, and said, "You know, I'm sure they did, but I would never have been home when they would have been there. I know Steve loved to work in his yard on the weekends. The man would be out here all day either Saturday or Sunday, cutting, edging, pulling weeds, planting, you name it. My wife might remember, so when she wakes up, I'll see if she knows."

Just then, Susan stepped out of the garage in a bathrobe, wearing a puzzled look that just as quickly turned to worry. "Roger, honey, what's going on?"

"Well, looks like someone broke into the O'Bannion's house last night, and Deputy Jenkins was just asking about ..."

Susan's face contorted into a fearful grimace. "Oh, my God! How'd they get in the neighborhood? How'd they get past the security guard and the gate? Do you think they'll try to break into our house? My kids are asleep fifty feet from here!"

Roger glanced at the deputy with a look on his face that said it all. *Oh boy, now we've gone and done it. They'll be no living with her now.*

Deputy Jenkins' face had the same look. "Ma'am, I wouldn't be too worried about this type of crime. Most likely, it was just neighborhood kids, but we're going to look into any help that the—" he stopped mid-sentence and looked down at his notepad—"the O'Bannions might've hired and make sure it wasn't some kind of organized robbery."

Susan abruptly cut him off. "I doubt *any* of the kids in *this* neighborhood would dare do such a thing as break into a home. This isn't the ghetto; this is a wonderful subdivision with very good people living in it."

Roger knew where this was going, so he tried to save Deputy Jenkins. "Honey, as I was saying to Deputy Jenkins a minute ago, do you remember the name of the housekeepers that Michelle and Steve used?"

Still upset, Susan scrunched up her face in deep thought and said, "I think it was Honey-*something*. Honeywell? Honeyworth? I'm sure they're in the phone book. I still see their little vans around town."

Deputy Jenkins jotted this new morsel of information down and then addressed Susan. "Ma'am, did you hear anything last night? Maybe some muffled voices or a car door closing?"

She shook her head. "No, sir. As soon as my head hit the pillow, I was out, and that was about … eleven? Maybe 11:30?"

The deputy made another note, then asked Susan about the O'Bannions.

"Oh, they were a wonderful couple. Great neighbors, although Steve was hardly ever there. He worked at least as much as Roger does, but Michelle just couldn't seem to get used to the fact that a man has to work hard to provide for his family and himself."

Roger nodded his head. "I think Steve just couldn't ever quite work hard enough to make it all work. He wanted to keep up with the Jones', but I don't think he had the discipline he needed to make it. He was a hard charger, but he would just as quickly interrupt his day to come home and see Michelle for lunch as he would go work on the accounts he had for the company."

"And what was his business?" interrupted the deputy.

"Oh, he was a mortgage banker with First Atlanta. Steve and I used to talk when I'd see him out in the yard once in a while. I think he was just missing that killer instinct that he needed to create the life he and Michelle wanted."

Roger thought for a second and then added, "If the poor guy would've had a little more commitment, I bet he'd have saved the whole thing. His career, his marriage, the works. As it was, I guess he just wasn't focused enough."

Jenkins nodded, wrote a few more lines in his notebook, and then turned to the Alcotts. "I think that's all I need. My partner will be over here in a second to give you a case number for this incident. It'll be on one of our business cards, so you'll have a direct number for one of us. If you think of anything else, contractors who did work for the O'Bannions, delivery people, even door-to-door salespeople that might've been in the neighborhood recently, please let us know."

Jenkins turned to Susan. "And, ma'am, I wouldn't worry too much about this. I know your kids are right there in the house, but in my experience, these types of crimes are only ever done when the houses are empty. It's a big jump in the jail sentence from breaking into an empty home versus forced entry into an occupied house. We'll probably have an extra unit or two ride through in the next few nights, and your neighborhood security company will likely increase the timing of their patrols. Ya'll have a wonderful day."

Roger thanked the deputy, and Susan turned and went into the house. A moment later, Deputy Jenkins' partner walked over—Roger saw he was Deputy Perkins—and gave him a business card with the Cobb County Sheriff's Department logo on it with his number and extension written on it in neat block script. Perkins thanked Roger for his time that morning and explained that the listing agent had been notified of the break-in, and he expected that the realtor and Michelle O'Bannion would probably be arriving soon to secure the house from the deputies.

* * * *

Later that day, Roger found himself thinking about the O'Bannions. He knew Steve had worked hard to get the things that he and Michelle had, but more than once, Steve had confided in Roger that he couldn't understand why success cost so much.

Roger recalled Steve complaining no matter how hard he worked, by the time he paid for the house, his Infiniti, Michelle's Lexus, the memberships to the right clubs, and the lifestyle he had to demonstrate to his clients and company, he'd have been better off as a loan officer in South Georgia, where he'd gotten his start ten years earlier.

Despite thinking about the O'Bannions most of the day, it never occurred to Roger that even if he thought that Steve O'Bannion had somehow been a failure, Steve *was* Roger. The only difference was that Steve had opened his own eyes to the truth before it consumed him.

CHAPTER THREE

Things may come to those who wait, but only the things left by those who hustle.

—Abraham Lincoln

A beautiful Atlanta spring became a sultry Georgia summer in no time. Despite Susan's worries, nothing ever came from the break-in next door, and life in the Alcott's home continued as it had for years. Roger worked sixty or seventy hours each and every week and nearly every day while Susan and the twins dutifully went through baseball season, and Roger continued to miss his children's games.

The first day that Atlanta hit 90 degrees was May 14, and as he pulled into his driveway that evening, Roger noticed the for-sale sign next door was gone. Spring in the Deep South brings on a strong growing season, and even though a landscaping service had been taking care of the O'Bannions' house, shrubs, trees, and even weeds had begun to encroach on the once immaculately manicured landscaping.

The next morning as Roger pointed his Lexus toward another day at Alliant, he saw a new landscape-company truck pulling up in front of the O'Bannion's house, accompanied by a non-descript Chevrolet sedan.

Nice to see someone giving a damn about the property again, he thought as he made his way out of the neighborhood and into his daily commute. It would be another fourteen hours before he would think about it again.

That evening as he pulled into his driveway, Roger sat dumbfounded at the changes he saw in the O'Bannions' yard.

The hedge down the long driveway so lovingly cared for by Steve O'Bannion was gone, all of it either cut back or pulled out; the fruit trees Steve had nurtured in the front yard, along with the array of evergreens, were simply gone. Whoever was running this landscaping company was getting work done, that was for sure. In the failing light, it was difficult to see other changes, but Roger got the distinct sense that a lot of men had put in a lot of time that day.

The next morning, he could see the fullest extent of the carnage. In fact, the house looked, well—*naked*. On the other hand, Roger discovered, with all the shrubbery out of the way, they had been hiding a secret—invading green mildew on the siding, rust stains near the gutters, and erosion along the downhill side of the driveway.

Roger figured the listing agent had probably convinced Michelle O'Bannion to spend a little money to improve the curb appeal of the house. *But I'll bet they didn't* expect *this,* he thought, looking at the house, its deferred maintenance now standing exposed to all.

"Better spend another thousand," he muttered to himself as he shook his head.

Right then, Roger heard the intense sound of a Diesel engine coming down the road and looked up to see the same sedan from the previous morning with what could only be described as a non-descript driver behind the wheel turning into the driveway. A late model pickup followed close behind, pulling a small enclosed trailer.

The logo on the truck and the trailer proudly announced that Sta-Clean Pressure Washing Services had arrived.

Another notification buzzed through on Roger's phone, and he knew it was time to quit wondering about neighborhood gossip and get to work. Whatever was going to happen at the O'Bannion house—make that the former O'Bannion house—was going to happen, and Roger, sitting around watching it like some neighborhood busybody, wasn't going to get it done any faster. It also wasn't going to get Roger's Alliant customers taken care of either.

The Lexus started up, the Bluetooth kicked on, and Roger started working the phones on his way to the office.

By the time he returned that evening, the darkness had hidden whatever progress the Sta-Clean team had made on the former O'Bannion house, but he found himself wondering how the house looked and what was going on. The for-sale sign was still not in place, and Roger thought, *Maybe the guy in the Chevy is the new owner, checking it out in a rental car while he gets it ready to move in.*

On his way back from the office early Saturday afternoon, Roger decided he would walk over and introduce himself to the guy in the Chevrolet and welcome him to the neighborhood. As he pulled up in his driveway, he looked for the gray sedan, but it was nowhere in sight. In its place were two white work vans with no company markings on them, but the ladder racks and the clutter on the dashboard told Roger both of them were clearly owned by tradesmen.

Tradesmen who were inside the house doing *something*?

On a *Saturday*?

But what? The damned house had always been immaculate whenever he and Susan had been over to visit Steve and Michelle. What could there be to fix?

Roger had heard the air conditioner kicking on in the last few months at the old house, so he didn't think that the interior could be eaten up with mold or mildew.

Since the Chevy was nowhere in sight, Roger dismissed the whole question and figured their new neighbor was just getting some new paint and maybe having the floors cleaned.

Just then, another notification buzzed on his phone, informing him all three deliveries he had orchestrated for Chicago had made it, and his curiosity about neighbors and Chevrolets disappeared. There was money to be made.

The next ten days saw more trucks, more vans, more deliveries. Susan mentioned that the Lowe's delivery truck had been there no less than three times in two days.

Roger was amazed that anyone could buy such a nice home and then spend so much more time and money on it. Steve and Michelle had probably priced the house a little too high, but every realtor who Roger knew subscribed to that philosophy: price high and haggle down to a price that is still too high while the prospective buyer thinks they got a good deal, and the two agents split a fee that neither of them really earned.

Real estate was a joke to Roger. Home ownership was part of the American dream, but the ways that real estate companies screwed the buyer *and* the seller? Shady bastards selling snake oil.

Roger started laughing to himself and thought, *And you bought the snake oil and the house. The whole damned thing. The biggest, baddest house in the neighborhood, the thirty-year mortgage, and a three-car garage, even though you only have two cars. Don't go throwing rocks, Rog.*

Roger and Susan actually had cut a good deal on their home. It had been a builder's spec house, and when that builder was struggling for cash in the midst of the real estate meltdown, Roger and Susan were able to buy a lot of house for the money. When all the other homes in the neighborhood had been selling new for over $475,000, the Alcotts had offered $400,000 and gotten a yes. The downside is that they had put up a huge down payment, nearly $80,000 from Roger's 401(k). That had been five years ago, and now that the market had rebounded, Roger figured they had a lot of equity in the house. One of these days, he should refinance it to a fifteen-year loan, but when would he find the time to do *that* research?

He flipped through the day's mail. The usual deluge of credit card bills, the bill for Susan's Range Rover, and the Verizon phone bill was there. The twins had been pestering their parents for a few months now about getting their own phones, and Roger knew what that meant—another two hundred bucks gone each month, plus the damned data overages and charges he knew would show up when Brent and Chris got on whatever social media was popular with pre-teens that week.

Roger sighed and made a mental note to call his friend, Billy Johnson, an agent who lived in the neighborhood, and find out what the O'Bannion's had gotten for the house. He knew they had it listed at half a million—*half a million dollars*—but he was sure they wouldn't have gotten that kind of money for it.

Who drops a half million bucks and then spends the next two weeks having a bunch of work done on a practically new home? Roger asked it in his mind, but as he did so, he was looking out the kitchen window at the now darkened house next door.

He reflected that what *he* needed was to quit hemorrhaging money each month. His Lexus, Susan's Range Rover, the MacMansion they lived in, the credit card debt. He could cover it all easily on his annual earnings—hell, he made nearly two hundred grand a year, but it went out just as fast as it came in.

The good news was that Alliant had restructured their bonus package for executives this year. Roger still had a monthly overage target, but now he also had quarterly and additional yearly bonuses. Nearly as soon as he had heard the news, he had been calculating what he could make based on his past performances, and the numbers were awfully nice and looked to be easy to make for his average output.

Ten grand a quarter, twenty-five grand at the end of the year. The voice in his head said it for him. *If I can get that, there's going to be some changes in how I—we—spend this money.*

CHAPTER FOUR

*Have the purchase price be so attractive that
even a mediocre sale gives good results.*

—Warren Buffett

The voice on the other end of the line was obviously happy to hear from Roger. Billy Johnson was one of the very few naturally gifted salespeople Roger had ever met. He'd made a small fortune as a real estate agent, and despite the many negative stereotypes that Roger had of agents in general, Billy had a disarming, aw-shucks aspect to his personality that made you like him, even if he was giving you bad news.

"Sure, Roger, I'll look it up. I hadn't been over on that side of the neighborhood for a few weeks, and even when I played the course last weekend, you can't quite see the O'Bannions' house from the closest hole. I would never have seen it if you didn't reach out to me."

"Thanks, Billy. Your family doing well?"

"Growing like weeds. My youngest boy starts kindergarten this fall! Can you believe it? Your people doing alright?" For some reason, Billy Johnson's south Georgia accent would ooze out at odd times, making a colloquial phrase like "your people" sound more like "yo' people" and "alright" into something that sounded closer to "a-ight."

He had called Billy to find out about the O'Bannion house and see who had bought it. That morning, he had passed a Mayflower moving van lumbering down his street and could only assume that his new neighbors might finally be ready to move in. He'd seen the grey Chevy a few times in the last week but never at a point when he could drop what he was doing to run over to snoop on his new neighbors.

"Gimme a few hours to get you the information on the sale, and I'll holler at you after supper." Billy's accent tried to make "get you" into "getchu" but didn't quite get there, and Roger could only assume that "supper" was what passed for lunch in the backwoods that Billy had grown up in. Roger thanked him and hung up his office line just as his secretary rang through that Maryville Consolidated was on the other line with questions about billing.

Since Roger had only recently been able to capture that contract, he'd been handling them personally before passing them off to one of Alliant's regular logistics coordinators. For the next two hours, he worked tirelessly just as he did every day, and when Billy Johnson called him at 2:42 that afternoon, he had not stepped away from his desk once.

Billy started with his drawling, "Well, Rog, here's the deal. Michelle O'Bannion sold that house for cash. Ironically, she was the sole owner, and whether Steve had signed it over to her in a quit claim due to the divorce or that was the way it had been from the loan origination, I can't be sure. At any rate, an LLC, JG Limited, out of Alpharetta bought it for $375,000 cash. Not much else to tell."

Roger was dumbstruck. "Why is an LLC buying a house?"

Billy, anticipating the question, had obviously checked up on JG Limited. "Roger, they're a real estate investment company. From what I can find, they have rental homes all over the Atlanta area, but most of them are smaller houses. Starter homes, older neighborhoods. They did just sell a house in Horseshoe Bend for a little less than 800 grand."

"So, I guess I've got neighbors who are renting now? Is that what you're telling me? That's going to screw up the home prices in the subdivision. Hell, that sale probably cost me some money! The O'Bannion house was worth a helluva lot more than that!"

"Oh, I doubt that, Roger," Billy continued, "besides, you aren't going to be selling anytime soon. Your boys are still in middle school, and Alliant isn't going anywhere, and they damn sure aren't leaving a transportation hub like Atlanta."

Roger stopped himself, realizing that Billy was right. Alliant wouldn't leave Atlanta, and he and the rest of the family were pretty much planted in their home for the foreseeable future. So, what if the house next door was a rental now? His life was pretty well planned for the next decade. Work and more work.

"Well, I appreciate it, Billy. I guess I'll have to go next door and meet the new tenants this weekend."

"No problem, Rog. You need to come out and play a round with us soon. I'm finally getting my handicap down out of the atmosphere these days. In fact, two weeks ago, I broke eighty for the first time. How's your golf game?"

Roger laughed and thought about his dusty set of clubs in the garage at home. "I might break eighty on the front nine, Billy. Thanks, but I've got to run."

As Billy hung up the phone, he paused and thought, *Why scratch and claw yourself to the top of your company—hell, your industry's food chain—and not take time to smell the roses?* His uncle had been involved in shipping when Billy was a kid in Pembroke, Georgia, and the stress had killed him as a forty-four-year-old. *Piss on that. I'll show homes and sell them and work on 6% commissions.*

Ironically, Billy never did realize that he made more money selling real estate than Roger Alcott did as a regional sales manager.

CHAPTER FIVE

The good news is, we're not bankrupt.
The bad news is, we're close.

—Richard J. Codey

The hope and optimism that Roger had carried with him throughout the summer came to a sudden screeching halt on August 4 that year.

At 8:48 that morning, a tractor trailer, one of the few that actually carried the Alliant logo and name on it, driven by a contractor who had only recently been hired on, was seen running a minivan, driven by a mother with her three children, off the road. The driver, Bennet Lyons, didn't stop there.

Over the course of another 124 miles, he ran vehicles off the road, smashed through roadblocks that law enforcement had hastily thrown up to stop him, and in general, created the sort of public relations nightmare company owners and managers observe, and thank God it wasn't *their* employee.

CNN was covering it live from just after 9:40 that morning. Fox News cut to live coverage of the police chase seven minutes later.

The server supporting Alliant's network was overwhelmed by the number of visitors to Alliant's website and crashed at 10:37 a.m.

News outlets calling the home office in Atlanta had overwhelmed the VoIP and PBX phone systems by 11:20 a.m.

By 12:13 p.m. that day, Bennet Lyons had been killed by North Carolina State Troopers in a shootout documented by no less than three local news agencies and dozens of private citizens' cell phones. He had caused hundreds of thousands of dollars in property damage and the deaths of twelve people.

While that should have been rock bottom, it wasn't. With few political footballs to toss, major news outlets took up the mantle of the victims and began digging into logistics companies, the trucking industry, and Alliant Logistics specifically. Experts were called in, and no less than six news agencies were still on the site of the shootout twenty-four hours after the wreckage had been hauled off and cleanup crews were busy rebuilding the guardrail.

Within the day, Alliant's stock price plunged from $28 a share to less than $5. Within two days, forty-six of Roger's sixty-eight major accounts had cancelled or suspended their contracts with Alliant. Nine more had called or emailed Roger to inform him their attorneys were reviewing their current drayage contracts with Alliant and were considering cancelling.

Fortunately, Alliant had properly documented all of their processes, and Bennet Lyons had never had any kind of criminal history. He had never been arrested and had only one speeding ticket dating back to when he was a seventeen-year-old. Experts on mental health were interviewed, and the long-haul trucking industry was endlessly examined twenty-four hours a day on CNN, MSNBC, Fox, and of course, talk radio.

Alliant having all their legal ducks in a row didn't stop the media coverage, though. With no easy way to explain why the man had literally snapped, the media dug into the industry, using Alliant as the tip of the sword. Five days later when the news hounds should have been sniffing around for something new, they were all invited to a press conference at the North Carolina state capitol, where a heretofore unknown ambulance chasing attorney announced that, on behalf of the victims' families, he had filed a lawsuit against Alliant, Bennet Lyon's estate (what little there was of it), and no less than three different Department of Transportations.

Total price? Two hundred million dollars.

The next week, the cover of *Time* magazine carried the picture of the truck and the carnage Lyons had left in his wake with the title "Highway of Death." The Alliant logo was clearly visible on the cover.

In a sea of low points, there simply weren't any high points.

One by one and day by day, Roger lost accounts or had to work the phones like a brand-new shipping agent on his first job. He certainly had the skills to do it. He'd scratched and clawed his way to the top doing just that, but the numbers simply weren't there.

He found himself practically begging companies to let him haul six loads of lettuce—*lettuce*—to Kansas City.

All around him, the rats were leaving the ship. Six days after the initial wreck, three of the nine sales executives that comprised Alliant's team had left, and two more had taken a vacation. The regular employees—the ones who actually did the work at Alliant—were still largely intact, but the rumor mill was ripe with ideas: the Feds were going to shut down Alliant; Alliant had paid off the DOT to save themselves; the Georgia DOT was tapping Alliant's phones.

Roger heard all of these and paid them no mind. He'd learned long ago that rumors were just that, and employees always had some kind of scuttlebutt in the break rooms. On the other hand, on the evening of August 16 when he checked his email before going to bed, he was surprised to see one from Alliant's COO, Clayton Fredericks, asking him to join him for a private meeting the next morning at 8:15 in the office.

Fredericks never got to work before 9:00 a.m., and he never sent personal emails. Any email Clayton sent inevitably originated from his business account or his secretary. The fact that Roger was getting one from him late in the evening and asking for him to join him at a time when the man was rarely seen in the office would have been strange in any circumstance; now, though? Who knew …?

It took Roger Alcott a long time to fall asleep that night.

CHAPTER SIX

We cannot make good news out of bad practice.

—Edward R. Murrow

At five minutes after seven the next morning, Roger pulled up in the parking lot of Alliant Logistics. He knew Fredericks wouldn't be in yet, but he usually got to work by quarter after seven at the latest, and today, while promising an unprecedented meeting with the COO, he still had work to be done.

Roger nodded to the security guard in the lobby and made his way up to his office on the third floor.

Nearly every day, he followed the same routine: come in and make a pot of coffee since he was the first one in and then check in on emails and what his clients needed in the next two days—deliveries, billing, you name it.

The nosedive that Alliant had suffered didn't change Roger's morning routine, but he certainly didn't have to spend as much time verifying what his contracts had delivered or would be delivering that day.

At 8:07, Roger's desk phone buzzed—it was Clayton Fredericks. He'd just gotten into the office; could Roger come in a few minutes early?

As he took the elevator up to the fourth floor to meet Fredericks, Roger couldn't help but think that even though he'd done nothing wrong, he was somehow in trouble. As he knocked on Fredericks' door, a deep, hearty voice called out, "Come on in, Roger!"

Clayton Fredericks was a huge man. He'd played football for Vince Dooley at the University of Georgia. Even though he had already graduated by the time UGA won the National Championship in 1980, his association with the program had opened doors for him as a young man, allowing him to quickly climb various ladders in the newly deregulated trucking business in the 1980s in the southern United States.

He'd come to work at Alliant in 1997 and would probably retire from the company in a few more years, but in the meantime, he represented everything you could want in a chief operations officer. Clayton Fredericks stood six-and-a-half-feet tall, weighed nearly 280 pounds—none of it fat—and had a head full of close-cropped silver hair.

He was as comfortable discussing four-wheel drive pickup trucks with a teamster as he was sharing his thoughts on the latest play he and his wife had seen at the Fox Theatre. Unlike many C-level executives Roger had dealt with through the years, Clayton Fredericks knew his business and his industry inside out.

"Roger," said Fredericks, extending his hand to the other man, "thanks for coming to see me. How are Susan, Chris, and Brent?"

"They're doing fine, Clayton, doing fine. The boys are growing up, and Susan keeps putting up with all of us, so I can't complain."

Fredericks pointed to the two chairs beside the bookcase in his office and indicated he should take a seat. "Roger, I know you're even busier than I am, so I'm not going to waste your time. All this PR we're getting is kicking us in the crotch."

"Yes, sir, it's a tough storm to weather."

"Tell me, how many accounts have you lost?"

Roger cringed at the thought, recovered, and looked at his boss. "Right now? Fifty-two. Seven others have suspended operations for at least a few weeks while they sort out if their brand can handle being associated with us, and the remainder have all told me in no uncertain terms that if I ever bump one of their docks with an Alliant-badged truck, they won't load. I can send a contractor for the load, just not one of our fleet."

Fredericks let out a low whistle. "Well, I'll tell you, you're doing a helluva lot better than some of our guys. We've got—well—*had*—two that lost all of them. Younger guys, guys who hadn't built the relationships like you had. I'll bet you know what they did—cleaned out the desk and walked out.

"Overall, our legal team is telling us that the lawsuits are all losers, as we had plenty of documentation in place and no reasonable suspicion that Lyons would go crazy. It's going to cost us a few million in legal fees and wrangling, but they think we'll weather the storm."

Fredericks continued, "What's hurting us now is that nobody else has done something stupid. No fires out west, the president and politicians aren't passing any laws that get people worked up and cause the media to look at them, and there's no big storm about to hit the United States."

And then with an even more serious tone, he said, "What we need most of all is to be able to get off the front page."

The conversation was going into places that Roger simply didn't deal with. Public relations, the media, even the news. Why in the world had the man invited him here? To chat about the media circus that was engulfing Alliant? Roger was an executive—he did have a vested interest in the company's welfare, but he wasn't the one to be able to right this ship. Why did Clayton Fredericks want him to come to meet with him?

Fredericks glanced at his watch and seemed to catch himself. "Roger, I guess my point is this: Alliant is going to beat this, of that I've got no doubt. What I really need right now, though, is for our key players—men like you—to really step up and produce. I know you do that every day, and we want to acknowledge it."

Roger wondered what Frederickson would say next.

"Basically, Roger, I'd like to offer you the job of executive vice president of sales. I know we've considered it over the last three quarters, and I know it's not the best timing. In fact, it's terrible timing. You have a smaller staff, you'll still be doing a lot of what you do every day, but with more responsibility, and we don't even have the cash flow to give you the raise, and worst of all, right now, we can't even pay out this quarter's bonuses."

Great, thought Roger but still willing to listen.

"I am, though, prepared to make your raise and your bonus, when you hit it, retroactive to today, but it might be two or even three quarters before I can promise you'll see the money."

Fredericks looked Roger dead in the eye. "Roger, there's nobody else that I could feel comfortable asking to do this. You, me, and a handful of other people are the only thing standing between Alliant and bankruptcy. I need to know that you've got my back if you take this on."

Roger stood up, extended his hand, and replied, "Yes, sir, I'll do it. I'll step up. I'll produce, and I'll get this team to produce. Can I ask you one thing, though? Please, I can't pull this off without the assurance that the money is there. I'll carry the ball for two quarters, even three if I have to, but I need to know that it isn't just a pipe dream."

Fredericks smiled, took Roger's hand, and said, "I know. You have my word that as soon as we have the cash flow, your money is coming. I'll have Janice from HR fill out the paperwork and send you a copy to sign and a copy to keep. Roger, welcome to the C-level."

* * * *

Roger worked the rest of the day—and the days that followed—like a man possessed. He was turning things around. Gradually, the media coverage waned. There was an attempted coup in Central America and a series of demonstrations in the United States about minimum wage increases, and Alliant, Bennet Lyons, and the trucking industry simply ceased to grab attention.

Roger doubled down on restoring his canceled contracts and taking over and reaching out to the hundreds of companies that had walked away from Alliant in the last three weeks.

… And he made progress.

Eight days after meeting with Fredericks, Roger had restored or reclaimed twenty-four contracts and decided to leave the office at 7:30 p.m.

As he made his way home, he realized it was the first time he'd been home before dark in nearly three weeks. As he pulled up in his driveway, he saw an older man walking down the steps at the former O'Bannion house.

Must be the new owner finally, he thought, then walked into his house.

CHAPTER SEVEN

Financial freedom is available to those
who learn about it and work for it.

—Robert Kiyosaki

Roger walked in expecting to find Susan and the boys sitting at the dinner table. They usually ate between seven and eight, and sometimes he could even make it home by then. Today, though, there was no evidence that anyone had eaten anything in his house.

Susan's car was there, but nobody was home. Just then, Susan walked downstairs. "Roger, I've got to talk to you."

"Hey, baby, how are you? What's wrong? Where are the boys?" He fairly stammered it all out as his brain tried to put all the pieces together.

"The boys are fine. They're at Jackson's house down the street. I need to talk to you."

Roger looked at Susan, and she looked fine, but she was certainly acting strange. Was this about a divorce? Was she seeing someone else? What the hell was going on?

"Roger, honey, we're broke."

Roger had a confused look on his face, and Susan looked him right in the eye. "The check for the mortgage bounced. The bank called me today. I paid all the bills like normal this week, and even though I hadn't seen your bonus check hit the account, I figured it would be deposited by the time the others cleared."

A single tear welled in Susan's right eye. "I didn't know. There isn't a check, is there? There isn't a raise, or a bonus, or anything from Alliant for this promotion. There's just less of you for me. Less of you for our boys. Alliant didn't even have to buy your time—you just gave it to them."

Roger was caught. This wasn't like Susan. She knew how hard he worked, and she knew the price of their lifestyle. She knew that if her family was going to have nice things, somebody had to earn the money for them.

Until just now, Roger never thought Susan cared about the hours. He opened his mouth to say something, and she put her finger to it, shushing him.

"Roger, I know you. I've known you for years. I know the man you are, and I know the drive you've always demonstrated. You've led from the front. And all these years, I've sat back and taken care of the boys, dragged them all over, to this practice, to this event, to this function. I've made the excuses to the other parents and in plenty of ways. I've been complacent in this too. I don't work, I drive an expensive car, I spend a lot of money to decorate this house."

Susan sighed. "Roger, I'm not some gold digger, you know that. I don't really care what I drive or even where we live. But I can't stand the thought of you trading me and our kids for nothing."

Roger, usually completely in control in nearly any situation, was caught off guard by this entire conversation. He stammered out, "Susan, you know that I have to do what I can do to make the best of this nonsense that happened! I didn't run those people over. I'm trying to save my career and this company. They asked me to make a sacrifice, and I expect they'll help ..."

Susan, normally quiet and refined, turned to Roger and in a hushed voice, said, "Roger, if you have to sacrifice us, at least make it for a golden idol ..." and then the verbal fireworks really began.

* * * *

Twenty-five minutes later, the screaming had died away, and two sensible people who had known each other for two decades finally began speaking as grown adults again. Roger wouldn't—and couldn't—budge on his decision to help rebuild Alliant, and Susan still couldn't understand why Roger felt he needed to stay on what she thought was a sinking ship.

They had, however, gotten the more pressing matters of finance squared away. Susan would call all their creditors and explain what had happened and see if they could pay the current balances due in the next two weeks. Roger's next check would easily cover all the outstanding debts, and the family would simply have to be conservative with their money this next month.

Despite a short-term solution to a much larger problem, he was still upset and decided to go out and take a walk in the neighborhood to help clear his mind and regain some focus. Little did he know that those next few miles would change the course of his life forever.

CHAPTER EIGHT

I'm a big advocate of financial intelligence.

—Daymond John

Roger walked out of his house into the oppressive heat that was late summer in Atlanta. The humidity was nearing ninety percent, but with so many days spent in the office with air conditioning, Roger found it to be a refreshing change. He had hardly left his own driveway when the sweat began to bead on his forehead.

He didn't really have a destination, but he found himself heading roughly in the direction of the lake and the shared dock of the neighborhood. The biggest downside of such a walk was that the return home was nearly all uphill.

As he walked, he found himself struggling with the fight he and Susan had just had. Sure, they'd had differences about money, but those had been relatively rare in the last decade. Personally, Roger had few hobbies, but he did refuse to wear cheap clothes.

His closet was filled with suits and shirts from The Custom Shop out at Lenox Square, and he thought nothing of spending hundreds of dollars on a good pair of shoes.

The rest of the money, though? The cars, the house, the club, the hunting lease (where he rarely even spent time), the boys and all their activities? Roger saw those outlays collectively as *ours* and not *his*.

Damn! How could Susan blame him? Like he'd spent all the money on drugs, or booze, or some obscure hobby! Hell, when was the last time Roger had spent something on himself?

After a few minutes, he had an answer and recalled he'd been invited to attend a golf workshop at Chateau Elan two months ago. Five hundred dollars for the day, and he'd been able to work with a professional who'd spent over an hour helping Roger keep his head down and focus on his swing.

Of course, that was the last time Roger had touched a golf club, so by now, his body had forgotten the lessons he'd been taught.

"I guess I wasted *that*," he said as he continued down the street.

A hundred yards farther down the street, he could see the dock on the little twenty-two-acre lake that was the focal point of the community. There were three benches on the dock and a small playground area for children. He remembered pushing his boys on the swings when they'd first moved here, but it had been years since he'd done anything like that.

As he made his way to the dock, he noticed an older man sitting on the bench farthest out on the dock.

It was the man he'd seen leaving the house next door.

The man turned as he heard Roger's footsteps on the wooden slats of the dock, and he waved to Roger.

"How are you?"

Roger, ever the salesman, realized he was obviously talking to someone used to meeting strangers. "I'm doing alright. I'm Roger Alcott, and I think you're my new neighbor."

The man smiled. "I might just be. My wife and I just bought Michelle and Steve O'Bannion's old home. You're the gentleman in the Lexus on the west side?"

"Guilty as charged. Nice to meet you." And he extended his hand.

"I'm John Gerber, and my wife—who is obviously not here—is Patricia."

Gerber motioned for Roger to sit down and, at the same time, scooted over to make room. Roger, hot from the walk, plopped down heavily onto the bench.

"So, Mr. Gerber, you said you guys bought the house?" asked Roger, innocently thinking back to his conversation with Billy Johnson. "I'd heard that a rental company had bought it."

"Oh no, that's my company, and please, it's John. It's just easier for taxes to let the business buy the house and then run the business out of the house."

Roger had a puzzled look on his face, but he played it off. "I guess. I'm a corporate man, so I never really understood the ins and outs of the tax code. I keep my records and send it all to my accountant."

Gerber smiled. "Yes, I gathered that. I see you leave early in the morning and come rolling in after seven, sometimes after eight every night. You're a busy guy. What kind of business are you in?"

"Shipping and logistics. I've been doing it forever and thought I had it all sorted out. Here lately, though …" He let the sentence trail off.

John Gerber looked out over the lake. "I can scarcely imagine. As Americans, we love our gadgets and expect fully stocked shelves, but we are the first to cuss if we get behind a tractor trailer on the road. And all this nonsense on the news with that company—Allied? Alliant? Whomever that was with that road rage incident over in North Carolina? That's got to have made some real waves in your business."

Roger looked at John. "You don't know the half of it. I'm a sales executive—well, I *was* a sales executive for them. I took a promotion to executive vice president of sales for Alliant after the accident. It was our driver that did all that."

Roger thought for a moment and then added, "Looking back, that might not have been the smartest move on my part."

John laughed the hearty chuckle of a happy man, looked at Roger, and said, "So, when all the others ran away from the problem, you ran to it?"

"I guess you could say that. It seemed like the right thing to do. My boss called me in and made the offer, but our business was absolutely crushed by that incident. He gave me the job, but the company has killed all the bonuses for the next two quarters, and I also didn't get any kind of a raise out of the deal."

Gerber looked at him. "But that didn't stop you, did it? I mean, you jumped right into the job, thinking how you could change things, make them better, somehow use sheer willpower to drag Alliant back. Didn't you?"

"I guess I did. I've always been driven, from the first day I ever worked. I knew—hell, I know—that if I just keep grinding, I'll get what I want. I'll have the things that my family needs and the means to afford whatever we want. I've spent my career doing that, and I've never failed at it once. Today, though, it kinda sank in that I might have bitten off more than I can chew."

If anything, the smile on Gerber's face grew broader. "You know, Roger, I've been there before. I thought that I could simply beat my will into the results I demanded, and that would somehow be enough. I was trying to keep up with the Jones', and it seemed like when I was still in the corporate world, I was in that tiny area of the pie chart that was not doing bad but could be doing better."

"I was always wanting and never having." Gerber shrugged his shoulders. "I managed to escape that grind, though. Or at least part of me did. After my first wife left me, I sank myself into my work and promptly had a heart attack. Damn near killed me. I decided that working eighty hours a week for a company that would have my position filled before they'd sent flowers to my funeral was foolhardy, so I got out."

"What industry was that, John?"

"Oh, I was in the financial securities industry. Packaging and selling securities to buyers, really nerdy stuff. In fact, the same sort of stuff that got us all into that pickle a few years ago when the real estate market melted down. Fortunately, I was long gone a decade before that."

Roger stood up and faced John. "How do you do that? How did you simply get up and walk away from the only thing you knew how to do? How did you meet your financial obligations? How did you—or for that matter—how does anybody actually pull that off?"

"Well, it wasn't easy. I had to completely rethink what it meant to be financially responsible. Not to buy things on credit cards. To invest in myself and to buy things that had, and continued to have, value."

John went on, "In short, I had to quit being addicted to work and figure out how to be addicted to life, just not the life that you and I were likely told to believe in. You know, go to college, graduate, get a job, build a career, get married, buy a house with little money down and a thirty-year mortgage, buy two cars on five or six years' worth of credit payments?"

Roger was taking all that John was saying in.

"If you lumped all that nonsense together, what you get is a bigger lump. Come to think of it," John continued, "what you get is exactly what we have today—a bunch of people making upper-middle class incomes who can't afford to pay their own bills."

Roger blushed in the setting sun and looked at John. "You know, you're right. I walked down here today because my wife and I got into a squabble about money. I don't know why I needed to hear that or why you needed to tell me, but you just described me. But how the hell do I get out of it?"

John looked at him. "You just have to finally decide that living is more important than a career. In my case, while I was recovering from my heart attack, I

44

realized that despite having mountains of *stuff*—a car I didn't own, a house with very little equity, and a lot of things in that house bought on credit—I didn't *own* any of it. I made the decision, right or wrong, to get out from under that load of debt and madness. It took me nearly a year, because like so many of us living this weird American Dream of the early twenty-first century, I was making $200,000 a year and still only a paycheck or two away from being homeless."

Roger nodded with complete understanding.

"Think of it like this: we collectively say we're 'keeping up with the Jones,' but if you bought a new Mercedes tomorrow, there's always someone out there who just bought a new Maserati. You buy a boat; the guy down the street buys an airplane. It kinda seemed ridiculous when I actually got my arms around it all, and I made the decision to buy things that couldn't be eclipsed or amortized. Experiences, Roger. Relationships with family and friends. Investments in real property that can never depreciate."

The two men sat quietly for a few minutes, and then Roger spoke up. "John, I don't know why, but I know you're right—about the way we all sort of, collectively, spend money. But when we're this far into it, how do we ever get out? Until Susan and I … umm … well, oh hell, until an hour ago when we started this fight about money, I just figured that busting my ass was the best way."

John looked at him and simply said, "Roger, not everyone even *wants* to choose to change their lives or their careers. Most of us are addicted to the normalcy, no matter how good or bad that is. We want to know our kids are in school, we want to know that our car will start and that the lights will turn on. We want to be spoon fed the news that makes us feel better—or worse. In short, we don't want to think."

A smile flashed on John Gerber's face, and he finished, "It sounds like you are in the same place I was years ago. If you truly want change, you have to learn—or *re*learn—to live. Push yourself away from the desk and go and introduce yourself to the strangers you live with."

CHAPTER NINE

> *The only way you will ever permanently take control of your financial life is to dig deep and fix the root problem.*
>
> —Suze Orman

As late summer turned slowly to fall, Roger found himself thinking more and more about how his career, his finances, and what he'd come to think of as the financial lunacy of the middle class all had merged together into the mess he'd suddenly become aware of the day he and Susan had fought.

Despite the short-term stress that losing a monthly bonus had caused, he and Susan had faced the challenge and made it through without any late payments and, surprisingly, without the boys ever noticing they were eating at home more, having a few more casseroles on the table than usual.

In the midst of all this, at odd times during the day, Roger would catch himself looking out the window of his office at Alliant and wondering just what he would do if he didn't feel drawn to have to work seventy hours a week ... and he most certainly was doing that.

He'd been able to recapture some of the lost contracts because the lunacy of the incident had faded from memory. His schedule had remained a nearly constant seventy to seventy-five hours a week, including at least eight hours on the weekends, but he could see progress. What he needed was for the various agricultural harvests to finally start coming in—when produce in the Midwest and the Deep South had to be hauled by damn near anything with an engine. September and October were usually strong months for Alliant, and once November hit, retailers were scrambling to get Christmas goods into the stores.

It seemed that if nothing else, Bennett Lyons had picked the best time to have done the worst thing.

Still, the nagging feeling that there was more to this life than working twice the hours of most men just to make ends meet haunted Roger.

The second Tuesday of September, as Roger sat in the daily traffic congestion of the north side of Atlanta, he realized what was meant by a moment of clarity.

With some sort of mindless background music on the radio, he waited to receive a notification from two loads going into Jackson, and for the first time, he suddenly realized that all the people around him—thousands of other workers sitting on Interstate 285—were going *somewhere* to do *something* that helped them make a living.

Where the hell are they all going?

Looking in the rear-view mirror, a stern, slightly craggy face looked back at him, the reflection of a tired, humorless face.

He glanced at the car next to him, a late model BMW, and the young man was on the phone, smiling. On the other side, another young man drove an ancient Chevrolet, but despite the traffic that slowed down the commute, his face was a composite of relaxation.

In stark contrast was the woman behind Roger, whose face positively beamed stress and broadcasted wrath. Roger found it ironic that of the three, the oldest and best dressed seemed to be the angriest. He continued to stare at other drivers the entire way to work that morning and realized that while many of them certainly seemed to look intense, an equal number gave off the impression of happiness, even as they commuted to another day at the office.

Where the hell are they all going? How could so many people feel that a job—or a career or a business—wasn't a drag or a challenge to be beaten but a wholesome part of life? He didn't think he'd be able to answer such a question right at this moment, but he suddenly decided that if so many others—even the worker bees—could enjoy a career, he might be able to as well.

Five hours later, Roger was reminded of this question from his morning commute when he found himself digging through some of the oldest files he had lodged into the bottom of the oak filing cabinet he kept in the corner of his office. He'd heard through the collective logistics grapevine that an up-and-coming company out of Austin, Texas, had hired an old colleague, and that particular colleague had been actively reaching out to improve his current network of shippers.

Joseph Smith and Roger had shared a room at a logistics conference in Los Angeles six years prior. Even though they had only been paired together by happenstance, the two men had done some business together until Joseph had taken a promotion that carried him out of Roger's sphere of influence. Having heard that Joseph was back in the shipping industry, Roger determined that reaching out might be the perfect idea.

The only problem? He had lost Joseph's number, and when he called the listed number for the business in Austin, he was told, "Mr. Smith will not be in for the next ten days" due to handling and moving his family from Nashville to west Texas.

Roger was determined to get in ahead of anyone else, so he'd tried no less than three other ways he thought of to reach Smith, only to be thwarted.

Ever the optimist, he knew that if he could find the binder from the conference in L.A., he'd find Smith's number, hastily scrawled on one of the handouts from the conference.

Finally, after searching for ten minutes, he retrieved the binder and started flipping through the handouts. There it was in neat, block script: "Joseph Smith, 615/555-4582."

Just then, the phone on the desk rang, and he grabbed the paper and retreated to his desk. It was an agent in the St. Louis market, so Roger set down the paper with Smith's name on it and grabbed another to follow up with St. Louis.

He made his notes, he clicked the pen shut, and then he looked at the paper with Smith's name and number on it. And stopped.

At the top of the page was a picture of Steven Covey—the man who had given the keynote at the conference—and immediately below it was the title of the talk he'd given that day:

"Start with the End in Mind"

In a flash, all the work Roger had to do that day and all the work he'd done disappeared. Suddenly, without any prior understanding, he knew he could trade in this workaday world and paper-chasing career and create whatever he wanted for himself, for Susan, and for his children.

He just needed to "start with the end in mind." His mind wandered back to that long-ago keynote by Covey. Roger had been fascinated with what the man had shared that day and how closely aligned Covey's ideas about goal setting had really been to the ideas that Roger had in his business.

Suddenly, he realized that the same ideas he had used in building partnerships and success at the account level in business could be the same ones he used in reclaiming some of the ... what? Zest for life? Time with his children and family? A new career?

Abruptly, the sensible voice in his head took over and reminded him that he had better get Alliant salvaged before he thought about himself. Still, the little voice persisted, and Roger even heard it in his head as the voice of a young child, "Roger, all you have to do is decide what it is that *you* want. Write down the things you now know are important to you and then reverse-engineer the actions you have to take!"

"But I don't even know what that is ..." said Roger Alcott to his empty office.

CHAPTER TEN

If you find yourself in a hole, stop digging.

—Will Rogers

The quote from Steven Covey stuck with Roger throughout that week. He had, ultimately, caught up with Joseph Smith who assured Roger they could try to do business together in the coming months, but the real treasure in Roger's hunt that day had been the Covey quote. He made a conscious effort to leave work earlier than usual on Friday, although it was still 6:50 p.m. when he finally got home.

That evening, he tried to talk to Susan and awkwardly explain the things that were going on in his mind—money, career, family—but the discussion sounded disjointed and rambling even to his own ears.

Susan had listened patiently and offered her thoughts, but Roger realized that until he could clearly articulate *his* thoughts, he could never hope to sell Susan with random vignettes of goals. As a man who made his living in sales, he understood that communication is a key in everything, and if you don't understand what you're trying to sell—or even share—then it couldn't be processed by your audience if they didn't have some common understanding of the subject matter.

How do you describe the color of orange to a blind man?

Roger had often used that illustration to younger sales people when he was training them, and as he looked back on it now, he realized that until he could firmly grasp the vague inklings of change that were starting to occur in his mind, he could never share this with his wife.

"… And if I can't explain it to her—the one who put up with all this for all these years—how can I hope to live it?" he muttered to no one in particular as he sat alone on the back porch.

He looked over toward John Gerber's house and noticed his new neighbor sitting on his back porch, reading what looked like a book. He decided to go over and say hello.

Walking through the backyard, Roger waved and called hello as he crossed over the property line, and John looked up from his reading. He waved back and said, "Roger! Good to see you. Come sit down and join me."

As Roger slid into the comfortable wicker chair, he noticed the book Gerber had been reading was, of all things, Covey's *Spiritual Roots of Human Relations*. Roger had no idea what the book contained, but he thought its presence was awfully ironic.

"Tell me how things are going at Alliant. Since we met a few weeks ago, I've noticed the stock price is creeping back up again. Are things finally returning to some sort of normalcy?"

"Well," Roger started, "I don't know that we're anywhere close to normal, but we've quit digging ourselves deeper. The team in legal seems to think we'll beat most of the lawsuits, but they're still flying around. It might be years before all the chickens finally come to roost."

John laughed and said, "That certainly is how our legal system works. Forgive me for asking, but I assume that you and your family made it through the challenges you had last month too?"

He breathed a long sigh. "Well, John, it's weird that I can discuss this with a relative stranger and stumble all around it with my wife, but yes, we made it through. I hate to say it, but it's part of the reason I wanted to come over and speak with you. I mean, I don't want to make you my shrink or something, but our first chat really made some waves in my psyche and this week … well, I guess this week did too."

"What's on your mind, Roger?"

Roger, never a garrulous man or prone to gossip, suddenly began talking. He shared his observations from sitting in traffic, he shared his thoughts from chasing money the last month to make up the missed bonus, and he shared his frustrations at not being able to clearly elucidate to his wife what he was thinking about more and more.

Over the next twenty-three minutes, it never once occurred to Roger that he was sharing some of his deepest thoughts with a man he had met one time, although he came to understand in the following years that sometimes, it *was* easier to share with someone you've just met.

Just as Roger was running out of things to say, a petite older woman poked her head out the back door and said, "John, honey, dinner is about ten minutes away."

Roger blushed and suddenly realized that he had simply injected himself into John's day and home and felt the hot flush of embarrassment. Gerber quickly recognized it and just as quickly squashed it. "Patricia, honey, come out for a moment."

"Roger, this is my wife, Patricia; Patricia, this is Roger Alcott, Susan's husband next door."

Patricia, obviously used to surprises, smiled warmly. "Hello! It's so nice to meet you! Susan came over a few weeks ago to welcome us to the neighborhood, and John said you guys had met while he was walking. I'm so happy to meet you." She shook his hand demurely but gave the impression that she was one of the most genuine people Roger had ever met.

"Roger just stopped by to share some things about his job that he and I had talked about a few weeks ago. I'm sure Susan is taking care of dinner, but I'd be a terrible host if I didn't ask you to dine with us tonight."

Alcott smiled and passed on the invitation. Susan had cooked dinner for him and the boys, but figuring that Roger wouldn't be home until late, had left his plate in the refrigerator. She, Chris, and Brent were at the boys' football practice.

"Thanks, John, but Susan already has dinner ready for me. If there's time this weekend, though, I'd like to ask you a few things. Let me get out of your hair for the night, and ya'll enjoy your dinner.

"It's a pleasure to meet you, Patricia, and maybe one weekend soon we can have you and John over for dinner at our house. Have a nice evening."

Roger returned home through the backyard and retrieved his dinner from the refrigerator. Susan loved to cook, and tonight's meal was Swiss steak, one of his favorites. Roger heated it up in the microwave, sat down at the kitchen table, and mindlessly scrolled through the newsfeed on his iPad. He finished his meal, washed his plates, and was idly thinking about going for a walk when there was a knock at his back door.

It was John Gerber.

"Roger, I'm sorry our conversation was cut short. Patricia has gone off to play bridge with the ladies at the clubhouse this evening, and I'm sitting at home with few plans, so I wondered if we might finish our chat? I got the impression you might still have something to say."

He let out a laugh and said, "John, I'm starting to believe you're psychic, and yes, there were a lot of things that I didn't say, but I'm still not sure how—or why—I need to share them with you. You might have all the solutions in the world that I need, but I should be thinking these things out for myself and not regurgitating them onto you."

The older man smiled and said simply, "Roger, I'll bet I've heard them all before. Let's sit out here because there's enough of a breeze to keep the bugs away, and I can't stand the idea of sitting at home waiting on Patricia."

For the next hour, the two men talked, Roger sharing the frustration he had only recently uncovered in his own life, and then John sharing how he had overcome some of those same frustrations.

John had decided years ago that he had to believe in the *Four Entrepreneurial Freedoms*, created by Dan Sullivan and the Strategic Coach®—Money, Time, Relationships, and Higher Purpose. While he convalesced from his heart attack, he had begun to think about how each of the four interacted with the others and how those resonated in his life and the lives of every person on the planet.

"In the end, Roger, the *Four Entrepreneurial Freedoms* are about *getting* free. I had to create passive streams of income, and I had to create effective ways to use time not only to make money but to allow me to be the person I wanted to be for those who care about me. I had to be able to engage with people that I choose to be around, and lastly, I had to have some reason for doing all of it, every day."

Thoughts were circling Roger's mind.

"As I looked around me at that time, I realized the wisest way to do that was to be my own boss and to begin investing in myself and in assets, not things. My business success has been predicated on real estate investment but not in the ways that many people think about it. There are a million ways to buy real estate, and most of them work."

Just then, the flash of headlights coming up Roger's driveway indicated that Susan and the boys were home. John stood up. "Roger, go enjoy your family and think of the *Four Entrepreneurial Freedoms* this weekend. In my experience, someone might need nearly a year to effectively change their mindsets, but it depends on where they are starting from. If you'd like, we can talk later on this weekend."

The two men shook hands, and Roger walked inside to his family.

CHAPTER ELEVEN

We become what we repeatedly do.

—Stephen Covey

Roger Alcott nearly jumped out of bed the next morning. It was Saturday, and though he didn't have many pressing issues to attend to at Alliant, he realized he could probably focus his attention better in the office. He elected to get dressed and go to the office, take care of some of the items he was attending to with a few clients, and then think about these pesky *Four Entrepreneurial Freedoms* that John had described.

Three hours later, Roger quietly finished the tasks he needed to handle for Alliant and retrieved a fresh legal pad from the supply closet. Earlier in the week, he'd taken a few minutes after lunch to look up the quote from Steven Covey—"Begin with the end in mind"—and learn more about the back story of the quote.

Essentially, what Covey had taught was not only to reverse engineer your goals but also to actually write them down.

Based on his conversation with John the night before, Roger realized that Sullivan's *Four Entrepreneurial Freedoms* were no different. In fact, they were complimentary. As John had shared, by redefining your relationship with each of those Freedoms, a person had the ability to live a richer, fuller life *and* the ability to create whatever they wanted.

Roger, who always wrote in black ink with the Mont Blanc pen that Susan had given him for their first anniversary, picked up the pen, looked at it, and then put it down.

For some reason, it just didn't feel right, and he rooted around in his desk until he came up with a Zebra fine tip. Apparently, this new Roger was not interested in status symbols.

Across the top of the page, Roger wrote:

Begin with the End in Mind

He continued that on the next three pages, and under each, he wrote down one of the *Four Entrepreneurial Freedoms*.

And then, he stopped. What the hell was he supposed to do now?

"Money" stared back at him from the page, and he remembered that Gerber had said true Freedom with money meant that *all* of your income was passive. You—or your company—made it whether you were involved or not. Roger had always been involved in sales. Aside from his nickname as the *Terminator*, Roger had always considered himself a hunter with respect to sales—if you don't kill something, you don't eat. He'd long ago passed from a straight commissioned salesman into the realm of salary and bonus, but he was still a hard charger who could close anyone. But if he wasn't selling, how the hell could he make money?

He elected to defer on that part, but he did run numbers on how much passive income he would need to generate to maintain his current lifestyle. At the same time, he also looked at what that number had to be if he didn't have some of the current debt.

Gerber had said that he refused to finance a car, so he paid cash for what he drove. Roger had seen the impeccably clean late model Lincoln John drove and had to admire that the man paid cash for a car that, unlike Roger's Lexus and Susan's Range Rover, didn't suffer from depreciation and didn't cost nearly twice as much after paying on it for six years.

John had also said that too many people consume things of which they have no need. It was perfectly fine to have a big screen television, but it was senseless to buy it on credit or to buy one to replace a television that wasn't broken. Gerber insisted it was far smarter to buy assets, things that *couldn't* depreciate.

Roger made a few more notes under "Money" and then flipped the page.

"Relationships" stared back at him. What could that mean? Roger decided it meant whatever you wanted it to mean, but if you were free, then you could choose those. What did he want? Roger leaned back in his chair and slowly spun around to look at the Atlanta skyline out his window. He loved his wife and his kids, but he suddenly realized that his relationships with them were amazingly shallow.

He'd been an incredible provider for his family, but he no longer knew them. As he spun back around to his desk, the family picture on the left-hand side of his desk stared back at him, and he realized it had been taken fully seven years ago. The people in it were gone, replaced by the modern versions. Susan's hairstyle was different, and the five-year-old twins were a far cry from the young men who lived in his home now.

Immediately under "Relationships," he started writing real stream-of-consciousness style of stuff—husband, best friend, father—and then he crossed that out and wrote "Dad" in its place. He wrote for another ten minutes and then flipped the page to "Time."

Here, it seemed, was where the previous things came back—"Money" and "Relationships." They would be bought and paid for with "Time." For far too long, Roger suddenly realized, he had borrowed "Time" from his family, friends, and himself to earn "Money." In a flash, he suddenly saw what John Gerber had been talking about all along—how the *Four Entrepreneurial Freedoms* fed into, out of, and across one another in some spider web of a Venn diagram or the organization chart of a crazy man.

He flipped the page to confront the last of the *Four Entrepreneurial Freedoms*—"Higher Purpose."

Here, with his new-found epiphany, he saw that until now, the only "Higher Purpose" he had served were the very base ideals of the American dream of his grandfather's time, not the dream that he had had. He simply forgot to think about the legacy he was leaving, both for his family and for his life.

Roger suddenly realized that nearly every goal he'd set in the past five years had been short-term.

What the hell had he done? Roger was a pragmatic man, and while he did believe in God, or the Universe, or ... *something* ... that was pulling all the strings, he realized he had neglected to think about it for a long time.

He skipped down to the bottom of the page titled "Higher Purpose" and wrote in his own neat block script a line he remembered from a college literature class he had taken his Junior year:

> *What is a cynic? A man who knows the price*
> *of everything and the value of nothing.*

—Oscar Wilde

With that, Roger took the legal pad and the Zebra pen, placed them neatly into his briefcase, and got up to leave. As he did so, he stopped, sat back down, and pulled out his phone and called Susan.

When she answered, he smiled and spoke into the phone, "Susan, honey, where are you guys now? Great! Look, I'm done here at the office. Can I meet you guys for some lunch?" He felt almost lightheaded when his wife said yes, and in a few more sentences, they'd figured out where to meet. Roger Alcott left to meet Susan, Brent, and Chris for lunch for the first time in years.

CHAPTER TWELVE

*I have yet to hear a man ask for advice on
how to combine marriage and a career.*

—Gloria Steinem

As a practical man, Roger didn't ever notice that on a particular day in September, his life changed. Maybe *change* is too strong of a word. On that Saturday, Roger Alcott made a decision, subliminally at first, that would set him and his family on a path that would allow him—and those he cared most for—to live within the *Four Entrepreneurial Freedoms*. Years later, he finally understood how important that day had been, but the simple act of meeting his family for lunch changed everything.

Not the lunch, however, as it was simply a forgettable meal at Wendy's.

As they were walking out, though, Roger asked Susan if they could make some time to discuss things he had been thinking about and felt he could finally explain. At first, she looked startled, but then he explained he realized there was far more to this life that they'd created, and he was tired of being married to Alliant.

Almost as an afterthought, he added, "And I need a better picture of us as a family."

The next day was Sunday, and the boys walked over to their friend Brody's house to watch the Atlanta Falcons on television and do whatever it was that pre-teen boys do on a lazy Sunday afternoon. Roger and Susan sat on the back porch in the shade of the pines, and he began to lay out some of the things he had been thinking, using Dan Sullivan's *Four Entrepreneurial Freedoms* John mentioned as key points.

At first, Susan was unsure of how to act or how to process all the different things he was explaining to her. As a woman, she'd come to expect her husband to go off on tangents and "chase bumblebees," as her grandfather used to say, from time to time. After nearly an hour, she realized that the things Roger was saying had affected him far deeper than she'd first thought.

And she began to buy into it too.

As they'd scraped by financially the previous month, she'd felt a pang of guilt every time she paid a bill that she felt she'd caused. The Range Rover was the worst— over $750—and ultimately, she knew that nearly any car with four doors could do exactly what she asked the Rover to do. Sure, it was nice, but was it neces- sary? She smiled as she thought of the little Datsun she'd driven in college. She'd saved up her money to buy it, paid cash for it, and sold it four years later for exactly what she had first paid for it. Her father had jokingly said it was the best car she would likely ever own based on that one specific fact.

Nevertheless, the former bookkeeper in her began to come out, and as Roger had done the day before, Susan suddenly saw how using these *Four Entrepreneurial Freedoms* could change everything.

Even though the boys weren't in high school yet, she understood that they would be leaving in only a few more years, and where would that leave her? Sitting in an empty home with very little to do and married to a man she rarely saw but loved a great deal, that's where.

For the first time in twenty minutes, Susan spoke, "Roger, I'd like to ask a favor. I've listened to you now, and I agree 100%. Can I simply do my own *Four Entrepreneurial Freedoms*? I think anything that has inspired you this much means that I need to do the same thing, and we need to be on the same page together."

Roger, on a roll and not yet to his *close* in the discussion, knew enough to shut up.

"Of course. When do you want to do it? Maybe tomorrow when the house is quiet?"

Susan smiled. "No, Roger, tomorrow's out. I've got to help with PTA planning for the Fall Festival."

Roger, normally impossible to read, looked downtrodden, but then Susan smiled and said, "I'm going to do them right now. Can you give me some time? Maybe an hour or so?"

He hugged his wife and decided to take a walk.

Later that afternoon, Roger was sitting on the back porch, and Susan came outside. In her hands was the same legal pad Roger had used. She sat down on the chair opposite him and smiled. "Roger, I promise

I didn't look at what you'd written until after I had written down my own thoughts, but you and I seem to have a lot of the same ideas. I guess being stuck with each other so long means that we think alike."

Susan continued, "We're both hung up on money. Period. And you've said that John thinks that real financial freedom only comes with passive income?"

"That's what he's told me."

"Then, I guess we'll need to sort that out, won't we? I need to level with you; we pay too much for a lot of things. Last month, I guess I finally realized that, even though it has been in my mind for years. I guess the first real challenge I see is how do we replace two hundred thousand dollars? How do we save enough to buy assets that give us a truly passive income stream?"

"Susan, honey, that doesn't matter to me. You know I can work like a dog. What matters to me is the time and the relationships that I have to apply myself to reclaiming and rebuilding."

Susan's face scowled. "Roger, we're in this together. I want you to be happy with the path that you choose, but I also want *you*. I've watched as you worked eighty hours a week, and I've become practically a single parent when I needed to. You're my husband. You asked me to spend time discussing this with you, and I am. You want your version of the *Four Entrepreneurial Freedoms*, and so do I. A lot of what you wrote at the office yesterday rings true for me too. But there's one other thing, Roger. Selfishly, I want this so that I can recapture my time with you. *My* relationship with you. I want that for the boys too. They're getting old enough that they should be able to make memories with you about guy stuff—cars, engines, guns, football teams. I can't do that. I can Google the hell out of it, but I can't do that."

A single tear leaked out of her eye, as if punctuating the sentence.

Sitting there in the late September sun, Roger Alcott decided, come hell or high water, he was going to make this work. He wasn't sure how, but he was still certain of the outcome.

CHAPTER THIRTEEN

*To get rich, you have to be making
money while you're asleep.*

—David Bailey

Sunday quickly became Monday, and even though Susan and Roger had stopped short of creating a game plan for them to pursue the *Four Entrepreneurial Freedoms*, Susan jumped into the "Money" as soon as the house was empty Monday morning. She knew that ultimately, she and Roger had to learn how to create passive income to truly be free with regard to money, but she figured that getting a head start on managing money effectively couldn't hurt.

Using her skills as a bookkeeper, she began by listing all the bills they paid each month against all the income Roger brought home. One of her close friends, Deanna, had taken a crash course by Dave Ramsey a few years ago when the markets had crashed and had filled Susan's ears for months on the many items that Ramsey taught.

One of the things she remembered Deanna talking about was what Dave Ramsey had called the "Snowball Effect"—pay off your lowest debts first and then keep reinvesting those payments into the larger and larger debts. As Susan looked through the various fixed costs she and Roger had each month, she realized that they'd fallen into much deeper credit card issues than she'd ever believed. In fact, among the six cards, they had nearly $42,000 in credit card charges.

"Help me, Jesus!" she muttered under her breath.

At the same time, she also realized that the family actually spent a lot of money frivolously. With all the darting around she did for the boys, they ate out a lot, but she felt like she was in the grocery store every day. She looked down at that month's bank statement—in one three-week period, she had been in a grocery store or the local Walmart eighteen times.

Her bookkeeper's mind began to work overtime. This was simply wasted time, gas, and, she was sure, money. She might not be the breadwinner for the family, but she could damn sure write and stick to a budget.

And pay the bills on time.

And pay down some of this debt.

Three hours and five cups of tea later, Susan had created a monthly budget for the family. She would run the cupboard as close to bare as she could and take a page from her own mother—buy groceries once every two weeks. She put herself and Roger on an allowance for the month that would cover any incidentals and gas, and she left one thousand dollars of *extra* where she and Roger could get to it if needed.

Then, she started paying bills. It would be two more months before the first of the cards—two store-labeled credit cards Susan had applied for years ago—were paid off, but they each represented interest rates over 22%. After that, she'd work on the Capital One, the Mastercard, and the two Visa cards, in that order. She still didn't have an answer on how to deal with the damned cars, but she'd burn that bridge when the time came.

It was nearing three o'clock when Susan got up from the table and began to organize her notes to share with Roger later that evening. She had to pick up the boys and get them ready for practice, but she'd realized that there really was more than enough money for them to begin pursuing these *Four Entrepreneurial Freedoms*.

She smiled at the thought of having Roger home more often.

Twenty-four miles away, Roger Alcott was smiling at the new picture of his family he'd placed on his desk from an ad-hoc selfie he'd taken at dinner the night before.

CHAPTER FOURTEEN

*The entrepreneur is essentially a visualizer
and actualizer. He can visualize
something, and when he visualizes it, he
sees exactly how to make it happen.*

—Robert L. Schwartz

While Susan fell back on her experience in bookkeeping
to establish a budget and begin the Alcott's journey
toward Freedom with Money, Roger began looking at
why his days took so long to execute.

Ironically, he didn't actually have time to begin
working on the "Time" component of the *Four
Entrepreneurial Freedoms* until Wednesday, but he
realized when he got home Monday night that Susan
was 100% on board with pursuing all of the *Freedoms*
and the promise they held for the Alcotts' lives.

Driving in to work Wednesday, Roger had the
realization that he could certainly account for all the

things he'd done in a day's work, but he'd never documented his actions to see where he was wasting time.

That morning, he started.

Turning over a clean sheet of paper on his legal pad—which he noted was getting used very often these days for what he now thought of as his next life—he took out the Zebra pen and laid it on the pad and started to work.

Every fifteen to thirty minutes, Roger wrote down what he had been doing. Not in great detail but enough that he could recreate his days from these notes. He intended to do this for at least two weeks and then begin to look for trends.

Saturday afternoon, he had remembered a lesson from another Gerber, Michael E. Gerber, author of *The E-Myth*, where readers had been asked to do an exercise similar to this and then characterize the actions they were taking.

If the action was about building the business, they cataloged the action with an "E" for Entrepreneurial. Managerial tasks were documented with an "M," and Technical tasks—the tasks of hourly employees or skilled labor—were given a "T." Just looking at the three days of documentation that he'd gotten, Roger saw that he spent entirely too much time on the technical tasks.

Analyzing his actions, he realized that many of the things he should be doing revolved around the relationships he was expected to build or rebuild, not just calling brokers and shippers. Yes, he needed to build relationships, but he didn't need to book freight.

He'd also noticed that he spent entirely too much time swamped with emails. Every hour at least, he was responding to one or more emails that didn't need an immediate response. Doing some quick math in his head, he realized that if he designated time to manage his emails, it would easily allow him to waste less time jumping back and forth. He also noted that inter-office emails dominated his inbox, and the vast majority of them were of little use to him as an executive.

That Monday, he set up an automated message in his email. Any sender would receive the message and instantly understand how and when to expect Roger to get back to them. Recipients would receive an instant reply that stated:

Hello—

I appreciate you reaching out to me, and I assure you, I will be happy to address your email ASAP. Due to the volume of business Alliant is currently handling, I've elected to concentrate on my day-to-day operations and creating reliable systems of communication in my office.

As a result of this, I'll be checking emails daily at 9:30 a.m., 1:30 p.m., and 4:30 p.m. If you feel this is an emergency, you can reach out to me via text or my office phone, both of which are listed in my signature.

Have a great day!

The effect was immediate and unexpected. Clayton Fredericks damned near knocked Roger's door off its hinges Tuesday morning at quarter after eleven.

"Roger, what the hell is this!" he stammered out, holding a printed copy of Roger's email response in his hands.

"Well, it's an email response to anyone who emails me so they'll know how to get ahold of me in an emergency and when they can expect a response from me about any particular email inquiry," Roger stated flatly.

"So, if we get a hotshot opportunity at 9:46 a.m., you won't know about it for two damned hours?"

"I guess so, Clayton. Which is why I reminded them of alternate ways to reach me."

"Roger, I think that's bad business. The few friends we've got in this business need to know they can depend on us and reach us anytime."

"Well, Clayton, I agree, and that's why I worded it the way I did and why I placed those particular times in the response. I haven't had a hotshot email after 8:45 a.m. in eighteen weeks."

"Roger, it better work, and it better not cost us a dime …" Fredericks let the sentence dangle, and Roger decided to let it go. He abruptly turned and was gone as quickly as he had appeared.

Roger smiled to himself, made a note on his legal pad, and decided to categorize this visit as an "M."

After two weeks of documenting everything he did each day, Roger began calling home all his lost sheep. He made sixteen copies of the organization chart and had one-on-one conversations with all his direct reports about how their job description explained the tasks they were responsible for. He also documented all of these conversations in writing.

He took at least an hour with each one of his people, making sure they understood exactly what they were supposed to be doing, the aspects of their job that Roger had been handling, and how that trend was now over. He broke these sixteen people into three teams and set up mandatory meetings for each one on either Wednesday, Thursday, or Friday mornings—at 8:30, not 9:00—and explained that since they were all paid hourly, they would be paid to be there, but they would most assuredly be there.

He was honest, and he was fair, but he made no bones about the fact that missing one of his meetings would be dealt with harshly. He was in the office no later than 7:30 a.m. daily, so he expected that grown adults could figure out how to meet this new scheduling standard.

One month after he decided to take action and reclaim his "Time" as a "Freedom," Roger came home on a Friday having worked only forty-eight hours that week. He did, though, work from the dining room table the next morning for three hours, but he did it wearing khakis and a comfortable t-shirt. That month, Roger's team hit every single critical control point on Alliant's annual goal—and Roger's unpaid bonus plan.

CHAPTER FIFTEEN

It's fine to celebrate success but it is more important to heed the lessons of failure.

—Bill Gates

October passed as quickly as any month Roger could ever remember. He was suddenly caught up in the boys' football practices, although he usually got there after it had started, and each Saturday morning, he, Susan, and the boys all piled in the Range Rover to go to Brent and Chris' games.

By the end of the month, he had taken to leaving his cell phone at home on the counter when they left, and he routinely left it in the car overnight.

It was a pleasant change.

Susan, ever vigilant about money, had doubled down on it and now was working on the next credit card. There had been seemingly no end to the creativity she had demonstrated with cooking meals the entire family enjoyed, and—at the same time—she had decided to trade in the Rover for something she felt was more appropriate for their goals. She wasn't quite ready to share her thoughts on buying a new—well, a *used*—SUV, but she'd been researching like crazy.

In short, Susan and Roger weren't finished with their studies into the *Four Entrepreneurial Freedoms*, but they had made tremendous headway into two of the four and had begun to realize how they were quietly making progress with "Relationships" and "Higher Purpose," even though they had not actively started working on either.

For Roger, someone who had always loved the fall, it was like he had suddenly awoken from a coma. Little things he hadn't noticed which had evaded him for years—Saturday morning breakfasts, listening to the Georgia game on the radio on Saturday afternoon, or even watching the standard late-season implosion of the Braves. Even going to bed at the same time as his wife.

The more he discovered—or remembered—the more he realized he'd squandered years away working for a company that could never reward him in the ways his family and his life could.

In the back of his mind, of course, the idea of completely passive income still eluded him, but if these last few weeks of applying himself to these *Four Entrepreneurial Freedoms* had created so much, imagine what a year of them could do. Or a decade.

Higher Purpose? He could see it reflected in his boys' eyes when he came home at night or when they ran off the field to hug him after practice. He could sense, in the back of his mind, that Higher Purpose slowly evolving. He realized his American dream might have been more of a nightmare, but he now understood that everything he wanted was within his grasp if he could actually visualize it and take action.

He wasn't even sure how that idea *could* work, but he had a friend from southern California who was into crystal gongs and meditation and all sorts of odd things who had shared with Roger his ideas on affirmations.

"Roger, I don't know *how* they work, but they do. The things you focus on expand, so you have to focus on the positive and understand that everything you want is out there," said his California friend. The problem, of course, had been that Roger hadn't asked the right questions.

In the last month, though, he had taken to trying to visualize a future where he and Susan made a passive income, where time was measured in memories with the people he cared about, and where the relationships he built were built on positive values and virtues, not business expediency.

On November 5, though, all that came crashing down. Roger walked into the office at 8:00 a.m.—another new change—only to find a Post-it® note stuck on his office door. It was from Clayton Fredericks and said only, "Can you come by my office when you get in?"

Roger opened his door, got his computer started, and then walked up to Fredericks' office.

The door was open, and he tapped lightly on it. "Clayton, you needed to see me?"

Fredericks looked up, surprised, and then smiled what had to be the worst forced smile ever broadcast. "Good morning, Roger. Yes, I did. Come on in."

Fredericks indicated the chair in front of his desk, not the somewhat warmer arrangement of the two opposing chairs on the side of the office that he had used when he'd sold Roger on the promotion a few months prior.

Roger sat down, and Fredericks started off.

"Roger, your team has been doing a helluva job these last six weeks. You've always had pretty good numbers, but you guys knocked it out of the park this last month. What happened?"

"Well, sir, I've just been trying to use some new ideas on managing their time and how our processes work here. You know, Clayton, we've got tons of systems at Alliant. All I've done is actually put them to work in ways that, well, that maybe we haven't used as effectively as we had before."

"Well, Roger, that's kind of the reason for our meeting this morning. You know, if I had to guess, I'd say you've only been working about fifty or fifty-five hours a week for the last month. Is that fair?"

He smiled. "No, sir, it's actually more like forty-seven or forty-eight, but you're right. I haven't had to put in the amount of time I used to."

"See," said the other man, "that's what I'm talking about! Leadership and using the tools we already have! That's why I needed to see you this morning, Roger."

Fredericks leaned over the desk, and his voice dropped lower, "Roger, I need you to teach these other executives that sort of logic. They work far too hard for a fraction of the results that you and your team are producing."

Roger was taken aback by the other man's candor. He wasn't sure what to make of the conversation so far, but he also realized he'd done an awful lot of work so far and gotten damned little financial benefit out of it.

"Clayton, honestly, I don't know if I can. I've had a sort of sea change in my life, and my time has become pretty valuable for me. I'm not doing anything that isn't already in the books, so it would seem anyone who wanted to exert change like this on their team or in their department could do just that. And honestly, Clayton, I've still not seen any kind of raise from the promotion two months ago."

Clayton Fredericks seemed suddenly to grow larger, and his face turned two shades of darker red. "Dammit, Roger! Where's your head! I told you we'd take care of that and that these were dire straits for the company! Do you think I'm rescinding on my word? That I've deceived you? That I lied? You bastard! Get out of my office!"

Roger, never one to shrink from adversity or even confrontation, was so shocked by Fredericks' outburst that he simply walked back to his office. He tried to rationalize it, understand it, and explain it, but no matter how he looked at it, he couldn't sort it out.

It was nearing lunchtime when a different Clayton Fredericks knocked on his door and offered an apology that almost, but not quite, sounded sincere.

"Roger, look, I'm sorry, but you know how much pressure we're all under right now. I shouldn't have blown up on you, but I really need a company man like you to help push us back to the top. I don't want your answer right now, but I really need you to think about it. Think about how you can spend time helping these other execs to rein in their time and make them more efficient."

Fredericks went on to say, "Can you do that for me? I mean, you've saved yourself, what, twenty hours a week? I'm just asking that you give Alliant some of that time back for a little while and help the team be more efficient."

For a fleeting moment, Roger contemplated telling him to go to hell, but he smiled, made a noncommittal nod of his head, and simply said, "I understand. Thanks, Clayton."

At 4:18 that afternoon, Roger watched from his office window as Clayton Fredericks walked out of the Alliant offices with his briefcase. Fredericks, not knowing he was being observed, was laughing and talking on his phone.

Roger Alcott found it ironic that his boss could ask him to work harder and longer but wouldn't do it himself. He remembered a small-time gangster he'd known as a kid in east Atlanta who once told him to "watch out for a cook who don't eat his own dinner." On his way home that evening, Roger decided he needed to pay John Gerber a visit and get to the bottom of this passive income question. He wasn't ready to abandon ship yet, but that day, he abandoned the faint hope he'd held that he could continue on the path offered by Alliant.

CHAPTER SIXTEEN

The question I ask myself almost every day is, "Am I doing the most important thing I could be doing?"

—Mark Zuckerberg

Roger knocked on the Gerbers' back door after dinner, but no one answered. His frustration turned to embarrassment as he realized that *he* was the one inserting *himself* into the man's Friday night, so why was he upset?

"I gotta remember who is doing who a favor here," he mumbled to himself as he walked back to his house. He smiled out at the cool evening and went inside to his family.

Sleep, when it finally came, was restless and fitful. Roger finally gave in about 3:30 a.m. and simply decided to get up and read in the living room. On a whim, he made a cup of tea and sat down in his easy chair, reading some eminently forgettable fiction book about soldiers fighting in the Boer War in South Africa.

At 5:45 a.m., Roger woke with a start and a sore back. He'd fallen asleep in his chair—something he rarely did—and as always, he woke up cramped. As he stood stretching in the living room, he noted the Gerbers' kitchen light was on. Then, the back-porch light flicked on, and the man walked out into the crisp November morning, nearly mimicking the stretches Roger had been doing only minutes before.

He decided there was no time like the present, so he slipped on his house shoes and poked his head out the door. "John! Everything alright?" he asked, loud enough, he hoped, to be heard, yet not too loud as to wake his family.

Gerber was obviously surprised because he nearly jumped out of his shoes, but he looked up and waved and said simply, "Good morning" in the same hushed tone Roger had used.

Roger edged closer to the end of the porch and said with a degree of hopefulness, "John, I've got to talk to you."

Gerber was either still asleep or unsure of what Roger said, but he motioned for Roger to come over. Roger slipped quietly through the yard and shook his hand.

"Everything okay, Roger?"

"Yes, fine, fine." And then, "Well, honestly, John, no. I barely slept last night, and I was wondering if I could talk to you today. I came by last night after dinner, but I guess you and Patricia were out."

"Actually, Patricia is out—she went to see her sister in Nashville two days ago, so I'm playing bachelor. I was here last night, but I might've been down in the basement and didn't hear you knock.

"What's on your mind, Roger? It isn't even six o'clock, so you obviously are bamboozled by something. Come in—the coffee's brewing. Let's have a cup and get the day started."

Roger nearly hugged the man, but came into the house, dutifully took the cup offered, and sat down at the table. He shared the event with Clayton Fredericks from the day before, he shared his and Susan's newly found success with the *Four Entrepreneurial Freedoms*, and he, somewhat sheepishly, even shared that he had been following his Californian buddy's idea of daily affirmations—writing down his intentions for the day each morning and noting at the end of the day the positives that had occurred as a result of his focus.

"Fifty in the morning when I get up, fifty at night when I go to bed. I even write the damned things out in a journal I keep. I've read Wallace D. Wattles' *The Science of Getting Rich* three times in the last month!"

Roger was on a roll. "John, I've changed nearly everything in my life as—and this is the crazy part—as a result of meeting you! Hell, I don't even really know what you do for a living. Susan and I are really getting into the *Four Entrepreneurial Freedoms* idea, and it's made a huge difference in how I'm living and the quality of life that I'm living. My relationships with my children, my relationships with my people at work. Everything is changing and so ... positive ... and then yesterday, this, this, *jackass,* just seemed to mitigate everything I've been doing."

John smiled the smile of a man who truly cared and leaned over the table. "Roger, you've just figured it out. That's the real part. The door is just opening for you. Let me explain."

Roger seemed to lean in a bit to make sure to hear every word John was saying.

"Roger, when I left the corporate world, I did so to protect my health. I had to find something that would allow me to effectively make money without giving me a heart attack. Well, another heart attack. As a manager, or a boss, your job should be to give heart attacks, not have them."

After what seemed like an awkward pause, he added, "That's a joke, Roger. You can laugh at it."

Roger, caught off-guard at the man's humor, suddenly saw the joke and laughed.

Gerber continued, "You've obviously done your homework. I mean, as you said, you identified where you were wasting time on things that weren't your ideal job. Unfortunately, you have to do that in a corporate structure, and that doesn't really allow you to exercise true entrepreneurial judgement. Oh, they want you to think freely, but they want you to speak the party line. If you have too much success, do you think they'll reward you? Of course not. What they'll do, if you absolutely kill it this year, is raise the standard bonus plan that you hit this year to make it harder next year. You realize that, don't you?"

Roger nodded his assent.

"So, Roger, I'm going to tell you something that will likely piss you off, but you need to hear it. Not because I have a bone to pick with you but because I think you're trying to fix something so broken that even if it was brand new and shiny, it could never be truly satisfying."

Roger seemed to lean even more for John's next words.

"You have to completely change your belief system. You—and millions of other people like you—have been led to believe that getting a good job—a career—is the game plan. Our parents told us that, our grandparents told us that, and the colleges and universities that we paid good money to for an education all told us that. It was true to an extent when America produced goods in factories but not as much today. The pension plan that made a career job so enticing for my dad is long gone. Now, though, you drag around a 401(k) that might pay you five cents on the dollar. What the hell is the attraction to that, Roger?"

Roger shrugged his shoulders. "John, I ..." He let the sentence trail off.

"Roger, you're a *wantrepreneur*. You want the good things that entrepreneurs have, but you're unwilling, or unable—I think unable—to do them. Until you unequivocally take responsibility for your life and your actions, then you can't make any progress. I assume you've heard of Jack Canfield, the *Chicken Soup for the Soul* author?"

Roger nodded.

"Then, you should be intimately familiar with the formula he teaches in much of what he teaches: 'E plus R equals O.' The *events* in your life plus the *responses* you take to those events equals the *outcome*. Period. Think about it like this—you've spent a tremendous amount of time fixing your job, but do you really even want that job? Have you thought to ask yourself that? Are you willing to take the responsibility that fixing Alliant actually brings?"

The other man at the table looked down into his coffee cup as though he expected to find the answer there. After a long minute, he spoke, "John, you're right. I've tried to fix a job and a career I'm no longer sure I like. I've realized that being able to provide value as a human being, a husband, a father, a friend is far more important than what I'd thought. And I've also realized that any job, any business, any career I go into is just replacing one set of problems with another and still effectively limiting the amount of money or freedom I have. John, you're not pissing me off; you're only telling me what I already know and am too damn scared to acknowledge."

John looked at Roger. "Then, it sounds like you need to figure out what to do with your life."

"So ... John, can I ask you a personal question?"

"Of course, although I certainly don't think you need permission."

"How did—or what did—you do or decide, or build, or whatever, to become involved in real estate?"

Gerber laughed at the awkwardness of the question but answered it seriously. "Well, the appeal to me was the freedom, of course. I did the math—I've always been good with numbers—and I realized that I could make a very good living owning properties and renting some of them out, selling some of them for a small profit to other investors, and in extreme cases, buying truly terrible properties and fully renovating them and selling them as newly restored."

Roger was intrigued.

"To do that, I needed three things. You've obviously heard me use the *Four Entrepreneurial Freedoms*, but for real estate, it was finding the Three Criticals—Deals, Money, and People."

Roger repeated the phrase back slowly, like a man savoring a testy dish.

"But Roger, there's a catch to real estate and the Three Criticals."

"And that is?" he asked.

"You have to have congruency with your *Four Entrepreneurial Freedoms*. Your wife, your family. They need to know, understand, and accept that life is going to change. In the beginning, you might be thin one month and flush the next, but ultimately, if you adopt real estate as a business strategy, you can finally get an M.B.A."

Roger looked confused. "No offense, John, but I've got one that I don't use already. I've got to go to school again? That seems counter intuitive."

John laughed. "Not a Master's, Roger, an M.B.A., a Massive Bank Account."

The two men talked for another twenty minutes, then Roger realized Susan and the boys would be getting up soon, and he had to get home before she got worried. Gerber explained that he'd only agree to share his ideas on real estate as a business model if Susan was one hundred percent onboard, so he invited Roger to bring Susan over that afternoon and discuss the matter.

At the back door, Gerber shook Roger's hand. "It will take you a year to do it right, but I think you might just be stubborn enough to learn how to do it."

CHAPTER SEVENTEEN

*The way to get started is to quit
talking and begin doing.*

—Walt Disney

Roger had gone home that morning and shared with
Susan what John Gerber had said and his invitation to
share his business model. Susan, ever the pragmatist,
thought it might be foolhardy, but she agreed. To her
way of thinking, real estate investing sounded like
snake oil or the job that some career criminal used to
cover up what he really did.

Not, she thought, that John Gerber was either, but
she found it hard to believe that anyone could make a
living in real estate who wasn't an agent, a broker, or a
builder. After all, those people were the ones that built,
bought, and sold houses, right? There was a structure
to buying a home in America—an agent showed you
a house, you decided to buy it, you went and got a

loan for it, and you bought it. The agent got paid, the agent's company and the broker took some of that, and the builder or the owner took the rest.

Simple.

How—or why—did anyone need to do that differently?

Susan's answer came about three minutes into John Gerber's discussion. Roger and Susan had come at 3:00 p.m., as invited, and were surprised to find that John had set up an impromptu classroom in his living room. He'd laid out two legal pads and two ballpoint pens—Roger wasn't shocked to find they were his now preferred Zebra brand—and had even placed a small dry erase board in front of the television. After the initial greetings were done, John began.

"The first question people always ask me when it comes to investing in real estate is, 'Why?' There is a thriving industry and a well-documented system for homeownership in this country, and nearly anyone who wants to own a home can simply go and buy one. They're wrong, of course."

Susan was surprised at John's remarks. *How could they be wrong?*

"There are systems at work all over the place that people have to get around—or those that are marginalized must work outside of—and, too, there are some people who simply don't like the current system. You and Susan paid about, what, $400,000 for your home?"

Roger coughed, looked at his wife, and said, "Well, yeah, I think that's right."

"It is; I looked it up this morning. No offense, but as a homeowner in the traditional American sense of the word—with a mortgage—you'll pay about $750,000 for that house over the life of the loan. Now, I know you put down a large down payment, so that helped, but some people just don't have that ability. Those are the folks that other real estate investors and I serve."

For the next two hours, John went into great depth about his experience with Deal, Money, and People, and the Alcotts suddenly saw how those items, combined with their new beliefs in the *Four Entrepreneurial Freedoms*, could transition Roger from Alliant to investing in real estate very quickly.

The key, of course, was John Gerber. He had opened a door to options Susan and Roger had never known. The idea of assigning contracts—that is, buying a house for one cash price and then selling the contract, not the house, for a larger amount without doing anything to the house—was completely foreign to the Alcotts, and their minds took the idea and ran with it.

Gerber called this *wholesaling*, and the idea was simple—find and put under contract a house in need of work and then reach out to known cash buyers who wanted to fix up properties and sell them. Apparently, Gerber did this several times a month, and the average profit for him was about $8,000 on any given house.

Next, he shared the idea of buying homes that were in nice condition and then renting them out. The idea, in this case, was to buy a home for cash and then place a renter into the property. Even if the investor still had to pay a mortgage on the property, the rent more than covered that and provided cash flow to the owner. Gerber shared that in his experience, any property should have at least $350-$500 in positive cash flow each month after the debts on the property were serviced. That cash flow, coupled with a few wholesale deals each month, allowed the investor to quickly pay off any debt on the homes he or she owned.

Here, John slowed down. "Do you guys see how quickly this can add up? Let's say you have a house that is cash flowing $300 per month. Now take that and multiply it by 12 months in a year—that's $3,600."

He'd written the equation on the dry erase board:

$$\$300 \times 12 = \$3,600$$

"Now, honestly, that's nice, but it isn't really worth your time. Let's talk about scaling that business model. Suppose you have 30 houses?" Again, John writes the equation on the board:

$$\$300 \times 12 = \$3,600 \times 30 = \$108,000$$

"Now, you see how that scales up considerably? At the same time, this simple exercise allows you to easily forecast what you need to eventually replace your current income. I guess it should be self-evident that if you own the homes free and clear, that cash flow rises considerably."

Susan raised her hand at that. "But John, what if you have to fix something? Last year, when the air conditioner went out, that cost us nearly $5,000. How do you account for that?"

"That's a good question, Susan. That's the importance of cash flow. Now, there are tax benefits for companies—and any real estate investor should be operating as a corporation—so if you are taking care of a rental property, you need to ensure that you have cash reserves to fall back on, but because it is an operating expense, the corporation that owns the property can realize some deductions as a result of fixing something like an air conditioner. Obviously, cash flow is a percentage game. I know that of the roughly three dozen properties I own, at least three could need a new air conditioner this year."

"Wow," said Susan.

"How do I arrive at that number? Simple math—the numbers tell us that home A/C units last roughly twelve to fifteen years. So, I extrapolate the data. The same as roofs, or appliances, or water heaters. Hell, in my warehouse, Tom keeps half a dozen water heaters we purchased when HD Supply went under last year."

John shared, again and again, and Roger was amazed at the man's openness. Finally, he raised his hand. "John, can I ask you a personal question?"

Gerber smiled at him. "Of course."

"Why would you give us all this? We'd be competing with you if I—we—could pull this off."

Gerber burst out laughing. "Roger, this is Atlanta, isn't it? How many millions of homes are here? I think you and Susan can be amazing investors, but I don't think that any one investor would ever corner the Atlanta market. May I speak freely, Roger?"

He looked at Gerber and smiled. "I thought you were."

"Roger, the simple fact is this—you're a company man. You're used to silos and corporate scarcity. Like we talked about this morning, if you do a great job this year, the company will raise the standards next year to virtually ensure that you don't have the same amount of success."

Then John said, "Are there people in this real estate world that feel like that? Of course. But the vast majority of us know each other and respect one another. Personally, I like smaller homes all on one level because my ideal renter is retired. They have a tendency not to throw wild parties or have small children that tear things up. A close friend of mine who is also an investor is the exact opposite. He wants starter homes in specific school districts that young parents will appreciate. If one of us finds a property through our marketing, then we might wholesale it to another investor. In fact, several investors like properties such as we both live in here in this community."

Susan shook her head. "Who would rent one of these homes? Why wouldn't they just buy?"

Gerber smiled again. "Well, Susan, there are professional athletes who live out of state but choose to rent in their new city before they buy. Others might be high-end consultants, or simply, families that have some credit challenges and would rather live in a nice neighborhood while they get re-established. There are actually two in this neighborhood."

Roger looked up. "Really?"

"Oh, yes. Too many times we think that real estate investment is some sort of seedy criminal enterprise forced on the disenfranchised. The truth is that for people who are motivated to earn, even a simple wholesaling strategy could yield a six-figure income in less than a year."

With that, Gerber stood up and approached the dry erase board.

As he did so, he asked if Roger or Susan had either read Robert Kiyosaki's *Rich Dad, Poor Dad*.

Roger remembered reading it years before, but aside from the fundamental idea of the title, he couldn't remember much from the book.

Gerber drew a large cross on the dry erase board and, from that, extended it out to create four boxes, two up and two down.

In the top left box, he wrote a capital "E."

In the box under it, he wrote a capital "S."

The top right box received a capital "B," and in the bottom right box, the man placed a capital "I."

"Well, guys, Robert Kiyosaki called this a Cash Flow Quadrant, and the idea is simple. 'E' is for an employee. In other words, you simply have a job. 'S' is for self-employed, and that means you merely own a job. 'B' means business owner, and that means you have taken that job and built a system that works for you. You might look up Michael E. Gerber's book, *The E-Myth Revisited*, to understand the intricacies of that challenge. And finally, there is 'I.'"

Roger sat back in his chair, taking in all this new information while John continued.

"'I' stands for investor. An investor is someone for whom the money works for them. It's truly passive income that means they can walk away from whatever they are doing for an indeterminate amount of time, and the money keeps working. At this level, in the real estate investment model, you have scores of homes all cash flowing positively and the team in place to manage the business. Each of the other three quadrants require varying degrees of work—and by that, I mean trading time for money. No offense, but 'I' is where I am today, and thus I'm more than willing to share in my knowledge. Roger, I know you've told me before that you've struggled with the idea of truly passive income. Does this—all this that I've covered in these last few hours—does this help you to understand a methodology for doing that?"

Susan interjected, "John, how long does all this take? I mean, buying homes, selling homes, contracts, rentals? How long? In the real world?"

"Susan, correct me if I'm wrong. You and Roger have been working on the *Four Entrepreneurial Freedoms*, right?"

"Well, yes."

"Then, in my experience, I'd say six to nine months. I've had protégé's who have never set foot outside of the office and had a true scarcity mindset that have successfully done it in a year. So, six months on the inside, nine on the outside. So, I have a question for you two."

Roger and Susan both leaned forward.

"Will you actually do this? Will you take what I've shared with you this afternoon and actually move it forward, or have I just been talking in vain?"

Roger spoke up first, "John, I will."

John looked at Susan. She looked nervously at Roger and said, "Yes, *we* will." As she did, she reached out and took her husband's hand.

The afternoon closed with John Gerber assigning the Alcotts homework. They were to each find three potential homes that could be purchased as well as finding ten real estate investors in the area. "Just look for the signs and call them; you'll be amazed at who might answer."

As they left Gerber's house, Roger asked, "What if we just bought, you know, a block? Or a small group of homes from another investor? Is that possible?"

"I'd say it is, Roger. That's how I bought my first fifteen homes." The man leaned against the door frame and smiled. "Here's a basic rule of thumb for you to go home and think about. Any property you intend to buy demands you understand an exit strategy first. Remember 'begin with the end in mind,' right?"

Roger nodded.

"So, if you are looking at a home needing a lot of repairs in an area that is hard to work up comps on, it's likely best to merely wholesale it and try to make a quick five to ten thousand on it. On the other hand, if you find a home that merely needs to be updated cosmetically—you know, carpet, paint, an updated kitchen and bathrooms, you should always consider trying to make those updates yourself in what I call a soft rehab, and those can often net you thirty grand."

Susan's mouth was slowly dropping open, and Roger's eyes were getting wider.

Gerber continued, "The soft rehabs can often be used as rentals in the long term, providing you exceptional cash flow *if* you own it free and clear or if you had long term financing in place from private sellers. Last year, my company did a number of wholesales, but also three soft rehabs, which by themselves netted us just short of one 100,000 in profits. That's in addition to the rental income we have in place."

Both Roger and Susan began to feel the excitement build.

"There is certainly a learning curve, but knowing *why* you want to do this—the *Four Entrepreneurial Freedoms*—is far more important than a surgical knowledge of the real estate business without passion."

CHAPTER EIGHTEEN

*You're either making money or you're not. If
you're not making money get out of the business.*

—Meredith Whitney

Despite the fact that they talked nearly nonstop the rest
of the evening, when they got ready for bed, neither
Roger nor Susan were able to fall asleep easily. Like
many couples who have been together a long time, each
knew the other was still awake, but neither said a word.

They were lost in their own thoughts.

Susan lay there thinking about the joys of having
a family that was all home at a decent hour and the
ideas of not worrying about Roger's health. Her friends
had husbands with all sorts of stress-related drama—
hypertension, heart attacks, drinking, antidepressants,
you name it. The ones who were healthy were still so
type A that the idea of a relaxing weekend was hard
to grasp. These were the men who were always on the

golf course on the weekends, or at the sporting clays course, or *somewhere*—and Susan knew that they would be there or at the damned office when the massive coronary hit their system, dropping dead while on a conference call.

She couldn't envision dealing with that, and here was a way out of it. She tossed and turned restlessly but never stopped to tell Roger what she was thinking.

On the other side of the bed, Roger was having nearly the same thoughts, only his revolved around the key that Gerber had shared with them that afternoon. *Passive income*. Here, finally, was a way to pull it all together.

For the price of an LLC and a few hundred dollars' worth of signs, he could be in business! He could control his own destiny!

* * * *

Roger awoke with a start four minutes before the alarm was set to go off. He'd been in the midst of a nightmare where he was trapped in his office, and Clayton Fredericks was banging on his door, demanding to be let in. Right before Roger had awakened, Fredericks had begun to ooze through the keyhole, like some kind of damned bad monster from a B-movie.

Four hours later, Roger had to smile because this was more prophetic than he could ever have imagined.

Nowadays, Roger wasn't the first one in the Alliant office, but when he got to work that day, there was an audible feeling of tension in the air.

Despite the headway that the survivors at Alliant still had made in the last two months, the ax was falling that Monday. An email from HR had explained that due to the continued financial challenges Alliant had faced, there would be layoffs, and executive-level compensation was being revised.

In quick order, the northwestern United States quadrant was shut down. Alliant had sold their contracts to another company in an effort to raise cash, and when the markets opened that Monday, Alliant stock tumbled ... again. Not quite as low as before, but it was bad.

And then the emails and phone calls started. Mike Franks, an old campaigner from the Jacksonville office, called to tell Roger he'd been cut, and his office was closed. Bradley Stevens knocked on Roger's door later to tell him that his position had been consolidated—whatever that meant—and he thought he'd just gotten a promotion but no raise.

Fully half a dozen people who directly reported to Roger were summarily downsized.

Clayton Fredericks was trying to run damage control by walking the hallways and spewing jargon about how Alliant had to "trim the fat to remain competitive." It was about 12:30 p.m. when he finally cornered Roger in the break room.

"Alcott, I'm hoping you'll understand how important this step is for us to keep Alliant viable."

"Yes sir, Clayton, I do. It's a damn shame you have to do it so close to the holidays. Christmas is less than seven weeks away."

"Roger, if we didn't take action right away, we couldn't last until Christmas."

"Well, Clayton, I guess I just don't get how cutting from the top line—the men and women, hell, the *divisions*, that create income—is going to save us. I mean, damn, the legal team is sucking thousands of dollars a week, and we've got to generate money to pay for that. We might be in the red, but at least we have cash flow." Roger's mind flashed to Gerber's cash flow ideas scrawled on the dry erase board. "Clayton, at the very least, we could push the legal bill into the next year and pay it down monthly."

"Roger, I think you just need to concentrate on growing your own team's sales and leave the corporate survival strategy to me and the board."

By three o'clock, Roger's stock options were back to virtually nothing, and his 401(k) had taken another hit. The hits had been coming all day long—total staffing size had been cut by twenty-five percent, and the last email Roger had opened had purportedly come from Clayton extolling the virtues of the decisions he and the board of directors had made and how this adversity was a necessary evil.

To Roger, it sounded like Communist-era propaganda. In disgust, he turned off the computer, but the insanity of the entire day, coupled with the incredible optimism that he'd felt yesterday, made him smile.

Suddenly, he felt like he was looking down at himself in his chair. The ceiling tiles pulled back, and his viewpoint was that of a tethered balloon floating upward. He looked down and saw himself, slouched in his chair, looking out the window. His floating-self looked out and saw the tall buildings of Midtown. Suddenly, floating-Roger realized that even just a few weeks ago today would have driven him crazy. Floating-Roger realized that neither him—floating, as he was, some fifty or sixty feet over the Alliant offices—nor the man in the chair, sitting-Roger—were watching the death throes of the company they were working for. He (they) were being pointed by God, or the universe, or *something* at the next steps in his (their) life.

He was still smiling when floating-Roger slammed back into sitting-Roger, and Cindy Hilliard, an administrative assistant for Roger and several other executives, coughed quietly at his door. She was clearly upset, but she looked at Roger and said, "I guess you're still with us, Mr. Alcott?"

"Yes, Cindy," Roger said, spinning his chair around. "I guess you and I made it through this purge."

"Yes, sir. You're the first person I've seen smile all day."

Roger hadn't spoken to anyone else that afternoon. Plenty of folks had simply left early, but others had obviously left to figure out what their next steps needed to be. It was obvious that Alliant was dying, and no one wanted to be the last one off the sinking ship, especially when Christmas was coming.

That night as Roger shared with Susan and the boys all the drama of the day, Susan caught the hint of negativity in Roger's voice.

She could tell that the boys were picking up on that tone, too, so she decided to speak up.

"Roger, the key in all this is to stay positive! I hear you doing your affirmations each morning, and I know you'll be doing them tonight before bed, but—" she looked at Brent and Chris—"the key in all this is to always remember to think in a positive sense. Don't say, 'I can't'—think in terms of 'How can I?'"

Susan continued, "... And it's like that in everything. Don't think that silliness of 'I can't afford something.' Think about 'How can I afford something?' Don't think in terms of 'I'll try.' Think in terms of 'I will.'"

Roger leaned into what his wife said next.

"Personally, I'm tired of all the negativity that Alliant is bringing, so let me share what I accomplished since you left this morning ..."

CHAPTER NINETEEN

*Making money is art and working is art
and good business is the best art.*

—Andy Warhol

Susan had gotten up that morning with Roger and the boys as usual, but she had arranged with Sally Johnson, the neighbor down the street, to pick the boys up from school.

She had dressed smartly in a pantsuit, deciding that this was her first day back to work and had moved her laptop, her teacup, and a legal pad into the dining room. Personally, she hated the formal dining room of her house—it was too big, and they simply never used it. Meals for her boys were usually hastily thrown together due to practice schedules or work challenges, so taking unused—or poorly used—space in the house and making that space into an office made perfect sense to her.

Working quickly and browsing the Internet soon identified well over a dozen companies in the north Atlanta area that did exactly what John Gerber had described. The ads and websites ranged from the pitiful to the professional, but the recurring theme was that their company would buy your house for cash, or if you didn't own it free and clear, they might be able to buy out the equity you did have.

Since she didn't have anything she could really offer these companies right now, she printed out the list, made her notes, and moved on to money.

Next, Susan tracked down the company, TriStar, that had handled her 401(k) when she'd been working. She'd never done anything with it, and even though there was only $12,000 in it—or so she thought, as she honestly hadn't looked at the statements in several months—John had mentioned the value of converting old assets like this into what he called a "self-directed Roth 401(k)." What a mouthful! Nevertheless, the young man on the other end of the phone understood completely, so she had started that process.

It would take some time, but they would draft the documents, and she'd be able to make the conversion through the company Gerber had mentioned. Susan fired off an email to them after she got off the phone with TriStar.

A quick call to Wells Fargo—the manager of Roger's 401(k) and the Alcott's joint IRA—and she and the banker discussed how they could take some of the money out of those accounts. She quickly learned that Roger could only take up to fifty percent of the value of his 401(k) while he was employed with Alliant, but since their IRA was a Roth, it allowed them some flexibility in both how they used it and what they used the money for.

... And how they paid it back.

By noon, Susan had a clear understanding of the process to pull out roughly $21,000 from the IRA and how they could access nearly $60,000 from the 401(k).

At 12:17 p.m., Susan suddenly remembered that in August when she'd been scrambling to make ends meet without Roger's bonus, she had spoken with First Atlanta about their mortgage. At the time, she had been worried about paying the mortgage on time, not mortgage products, but she decided to call them back.

Susan followed the auto-attendant's prompts until she finally got what she needed—a live person. In her sweetest voice, she asked the young man, James, about a home equity line of credit, or HELOC.

James politely went through the entire process and reviewed her information. Based on their payment history, their credit rating, and the relative value of the house, he determined they would qualify for at least $97,000 and possibly as much as $122,000.

Susan nearly passed out.

"James, let's move forward with this. I'd like to get as much as possible, you know, just in case."

"Yes ma'am. The process is pretty straightforward. You'll fill out the application I'm about to send you, and Mr. Alcott will have to sign it. It's actually signed electronically with DocuSign, so you don't even need to print it to sign. You'll send that back to us. We'll have to pull your credit, but the actual process is only a couple of business days. In the end, you'll have to go down to your local branch and sign the completed paperwork, but you can take distributions from that account online if you'd like."

He continued, "Now, Mrs. Alcott, once this account is opened, you'll basically have access to a credit card based on the equity in your home. First Atlanta won't dictate to what use you put those monies, but I am legally bound to tell you that you are, in effect, borrowing money from yourself. You aren't bound to use the money in this HELOC account; in fact, many people just like to have it there, in case they have an emergency. The money is already yours; in effect, it's what you and Mr. Alcott have saved in the ownership of your home. Do you understand that?"

"Yes, sir, James, I sure do."

"Alright, Mrs. Alcott, I'll send you the paperwork, and you can send it back when you have time. If we don't hear from you in seven business days, the application will become null and void, as a means of protecting your account information."

Susan got off of the phone and nearly burst out giggling. She and Roger weren't rich, but they did have money if they needed it. Why didn't anyone teach this sort of stuff?

Just then, a knock on the door interrupted her.

It was Patricia Gerber, back from her sister's and looking for a stray cat she'd been feeding in the neighborhood. Susan hadn't seen the cat, but she was so excited about her money adventures that she shared it with the other woman.

Patricia laughed with her and said, "You should try your credit cards too."

"How? I've never even heard of such a thing!"

"Oh, good grief, it's almost devious! Here's what you do—call your credit card company and go through all the technical auto-response mumbo-jumbo. Sooner or later, you get to a real live person, and then you ask them what your credit limit is and what interest rate you're paying."

Patricia began to laugh. "Here's the fun part. You just straight up say, 'I need to get an increase in my credit limit, and I'd like you to lower my interest rate. I keep seeing all these great deals advertised online and on the television, so I need you to help me out.' And then you just stop talking."

"What do they do?"

"Well, for starters, they'll usually ask you what you're going to do with the money, so I always tell them home improvements because we only use credit cards as *investment* cards. I just don't tell them *whose* home we're improving."

"And then what?"

"Inevitably, they'll say something like, 'At this time, Mrs. Gerber, we really can't help you out,' and so I hit them with a 'Hmmmmm'. Draw it out, just like that."

Susan smiled. "And then what?"

Smiling just a little bit, Patricia continued, "Now, I ask to speak to their boss. When I get them on the line, I hit them with the same exact phrase—all the way down to the 'Hmmmmm,' and that's usually when they give me the money or the lower interest rate, at least for six months."

Susan was shocked. "It's that easy?"

"Try it on all your cards and tell me if it works. Usually, I don't have to ask for the manager, but some-times I do. We've used that system so many times that it's second nature. We each call every one of our credit card companies once a quarter."

"But why do I want so much credit? I'm trying to stay away from credit card debt, Patricia. It's not helping us."

The other woman looked at Susan and smiled again. She reached out her hand and patted Susan's. "Honey, I never said you'd *use* that credit. But isn't it nice to have it and not need it? John and I have over $100,000 in credit card *credit* but no credit card *debt*. When a banker looks at our credit scores, he sees high limits and no debt. He sees fast repayment and no rolling credit card balances. That's why you have this. Besides, it's good for your credit score not to have more than 40% of your available credit being used any given month.

"Try it—say it exactly as I just told you—and then call me tonight to tell me what they told you. Now, I've gotta run and figure out who is feeding that kitty."

Susan closed the door and immediately felt something shift in her mind. She went and got her purse, pulled out her cards, and started calling each number for customer service on the back of the cards.

She stammered her way through Capital One, she realized, but they ended up giving her an extra $5,000 and lowered her interest rate for the next six months. Her next call to Mastercard yielded no less than a $10,000 increase, but they didn't budge on the interest rate. The next card out of the purse was a second Capital One, and they regretfully informed Susan that they could not increase her credit limit because she was at the maximum limit of their card system. They politely asked if she would like to speak to a New Accounts representative, and after a moment's hesitation, Susan said yes.

Fourteen minutes later, they indicated that Susan had qualified for a new card, no interest for one year, and a $23,000 credit limit. She thanked them, clarified when the new card would be sent, and hung up the phone.

She looked around the *dining room cum office* in disbelief. In the space of a few hours, she had created over $35,000 in new credit and had freed up over $100,000 in usable money for her and Roger to build out a real estate business that she still wasn't 100% clear on.

She looked through the door at the clock on the microwave. It wasn't even two in the afternoon. "If this is real estate, damn, I'm in!" she said to the empty house.

That night as she recounted her story to her three boys, she looked at her husband, still smarting from his terrible day at work, and simply said, "Roger, I'm in, and I want you to be. We can do this—everything John and Patricia have shared with us. I know it, and I think you're still figuring it out, but deep inside, you know it too. Don't let Alliant bring you down."

CHAPTER TWENTY

Don't be afraid to get creative and
experiment with your marketing.

—Mike Volpe

Tuesday morning dawned cold and clear, and after Susan dropped the boys off at school, she decided that her second day in the real estate business was going to be spent researching what John Gerber had called bandit signs.

The premise was simple, as she understood it. A real estate investor, like Gerber, would use a simple handwritten sign placed on various intersections to find motivated sellers and, in some cases, to help build his buyers list. Sometimes they had signs printed, but most of them were designed to look handwritten. "You want people to call thinking that you're selling a specific house, which of course, you *just* sold. Perhaps they'd like to look at another one you have," he'd said.

At first, Susan didn't get it. "But John, why wouldn't you simply advertise all your houses?"

John laughed. "Susan, honey, there might *never* have been a house in the first place. This is what we call a lead magnet—something to inspire people to call you. The vast majority of our business at JG Limited is now done with direct mail, but to jump start a real estate investor? Signs offer a very low cost of entry."

Susan looked unconvinced. "Direct mail? Isn't that just junk mail?"

Gerber laughed. "In some cases, yes, Susan, it is. But far from the circulars that you're likely used to seeing in your mailbox each day, a good direct mail program can target specific areas of a city, specific people in those areas, and even specific demographics within a zip code. For example, we work with a company that can provide us a list of homeowners—not renters, but *homeowners*—that have at least 70% equity in their homes. In some cases, you can only use the age of the loan, but in others, the data is available directly. It can simply depend on what agency you use. You'd be shocked at the seemingly obscure data that can be gleaned today."

Gerber barely took a breath. "So, instead of using bandit signs, my company can send thousands of pieces of direct mail—that look professional and are addressed to the homeowners—and generate far more responses than our signs used to do. Don't get me wrong. We'll still use signs, because in some markets, it's what the customers have been trained to look for, but for my money? Direct mail is the platform you want to evolve into using."

"So, why don't I ever see any in my mailbox?" Susan inquired.

Gerber laughed. "Well, for starters, you guys likely don't have enough equity in your homes, and frankly, my company doesn't target homes like we have here in the neighborhood."

Gerber continued by sharing that many investors still used signs despite the fact they were against local signage codes in many cities—hence the term bandit. An investor might put out fifty or a hundred signs around town on Friday after the local government offices closed down, leave them up all weekend to attract attention, and then gather them all back up early Monday morning before local code enforcement officers could take them down and destroy them. Since the signs were such an effective method of reaching potential buyers—whether investors or families—and reaching people who were truly motivated to sell, many investors simply left a few up all week long, figuring that the benefits outweighed the costs. No one, at least in recent memory, had been fined for leaving a sign up.

At first, Susan couldn't envision what Gerber had been describing. She was always in her car on the weekends, doing something, but she couldn't remember seeing a single one. John countered by asking, "Susan, how many Range Rovers did you see this weekend?"

"I don't know. Maybe three or four?"

"My point exactly, ma'am. You saw the Range Rovers because you drive a Range Rover. We're only going to see what we are looking for. The key to bandit signs is this—you want to attract investors by advertising that you have properties for sale, and you want to attract people that need to sell a home quickly. At the same time, you can use the information on the signs to help you build a list of potential buyers if you were wholesaling a house. Signs are sort of the real estate investor *Craigslist* while direct mail is a real estate investor *Match.com*."

Four miles from the boys' school, Susan finally saw her first sign. It was actually nicely printed, obviously by a print shop, and proudly announced, "We Buy Ugly Houses" at the top. Underneath was a phone number, and the third line contained an easy-to-remember website. Susan pulled over, grabbed her phone, and took a picture of the sign.

A few miles later, Susan spotted another one. This one was hand printed and advertised "3 bed/2 bath starter on 1 acre." The second line had "$59,000," and the third line had a local phone number. She noted that both signs were the same bright yellow color and wondered if the two were from the same company.

Ninety minutes later, Susan was nearly into Douglasville on the west side of Atlanta but had taken no less than seventeen pictures of bandit signs along the way.

And this was a Tuesday morning! She couldn't imagine what these intersections would look like on a Saturday!

Susan piloted the Range Rover back to Interstate 20 and began navigating back to the house on the north side of Atlanta. As she drove, she thought about what to do with the list she'd accumulated and how best to approach these people.

At home, she tried to think of the best time to call the various numbers she'd collected. She'd pulled all the numbers off the pictures and created a list of the numbers and websites she'd documented. Of the seventeen, it appeared there were actually eight companies or investors represented in her cross section.

Brewing up a cup of tea, she settled into her office, flipped open her legal pad, and decided that even if she wasn't sure what to ask, she was silly to let a phone call intimidate her.

She dialed the first number.

And got voicemail. A pleasant voice gave her the name of the company and told her that the house she was calling about had been sold yesterday, but the company had a variety of similar homes they could help her to find in the north Atlanta area, so please leave her name and number, and they'd call her back as soon as possible. She left a polite message with the information and called the next number.

Another voicemail! This one was slightly different, but the general message was the same. The house had been sold, but the company had multiple homes for sale in the metro area. Please leave her name and a contact number, and a member of their team would reach out to her ASAP.

Shrugging her shoulders, she left her name and number.

A third call, a third message. This one had been a "We Buy Ugly Houses" sign, and the young lady who answered was friendly and informative. Susan, taking a page from her own affirmations, told the young lady that she and Roger were newly started in wholesaling and would like to learn more about the company that was offering to buy these homes.

As soon as she said it, she regretted it because she realized the woman on the other end of the phone was only a gatekeeper. It was likely that she didn't have a clue about how the company worked, and if she passed along the message, she would probably screw it up.

To Susan's surprise, the woman said, "That's awesome! My husband and I got started as birddogs for my boss, and then after we had saved up some money, we started wholesaling too! In fact, we just did our first deal last month. Let me get your information, and I'm sure Mr. Franklin would be happy to meet with you all."

Susan almost dropped the phone. She wasn't used to people offering help. In fact, the country club crowd she was used to dealing with seemed to revel in other's misfortunes, or at least liked to gossip about it.

It seemed the more she opened her eyes to real estate investment, the more she found out that the people involved in it were open to helping others and expanding their network. She knew it wasn't all for altruism but for business, yet it was surely nice to meet people who weren't being such pricks about it.

She had an appointment with the hairdresser at 12:30, so she couldn't finish the list, but when she was done, she plopped back into her chair and kept dialing. The next number she dialed had been taken off an admittedly haggard-looking sign that had been handwritten.

This time, an older gentleman answered the phone and simply said, "Hello."

Susan was caught off guard. "Yes, sir, I'm calling about the house for sale? You had a sign at—she looked up the road—at the corner of Shadowlawn and Cobb Parkway?"

The man laughed the hearty chuckle of an old man. "My Heavens, I'd forgotten all about that sign. Young lady, my name is Louis Neiman, and I've been buying and selling homes for nearly two decades. I turned 74 a few months ago, and I'll be honest, I'm getting out of the business."

Susan sighed into the phone. "Well, Mr. Neiman, that stinks. My husband and I finally begin to understand real estate investment, and we're actively looking for buyers, and as soon as I've met you, you're leaving!" She laughed at her sarcasm, and Neiman did as well.

She liked the man and really wished she could add him to her and Roger's list of mentors.

Nonetheless, Susan and Louis chatted for nearly twenty minutes, and as the conversation was coming to a natural pause, Louis simply asked Susan if she and Roger would like to meet for dinner one night that week.

Caught off guard, she quickly agreed. Roger's Alliant schedule be damned. "Just say where, Mr. Neiman, and Roger and I can make it happen."

"Well, I assume you're on the north side?"

"Yes, sir, we're not far from Perimeter Mall."

"Perfect. How about Canoe? I have a standing reservation there on Thursdays at 7:00 p.m., so I'll call them and tell them to change my regular seat into a table for three. Since my wife passed, I've always challenged myself to continue to socialize, so I treat myself each week to two nice dinners in honor of her."

She was caught off guard again. "Mr. Neiman, I'm sorry for your loss."

"Susan, please, it's Louis, and don't worry about Jesse. She's in a better place, and honestly, she passed many years ago. She'll always be my wife, though, so I honor her and the things she enjoyed."

"Can I ask you a quick question, Susan? It sounds like you and Roger are quite serious about building this business. Are you more drawn to the wholesaling or the rental side of the industry?"

Susan said she honestly wasn't sure, but they were investigating and hoping to invest in both.

"Well, then let's talk about it Thursday at dinner. I've sold most of my properties, but the last couple dozen, I'm thinking about simply packaging and selling as a single portfolio. Perhaps it would be an investment you and Roger would be interested in. We'll chat about it in a few days. Thank you for your time, Susan."

"Louis, thank you *so* much."

Susan hung up the phone and shook her head at the amazing things that life could give you if you just looked.

CHAPTER TWENTY-ONE

*It's cheaper to buy a house and finance it
than it is to rent in many markets.*

—Barry Sternlicht

When Roger pulled into the garage, Susan nearly fell out of the door in her haste to tell him about her day. She recounted her bandit sign experiences and then shared her call with Louis Neiman.

She didn't have a lot to go on, but she hadn't been able to help herself—if Louis' two dozen homes were returning cash flow like John Gerber's model, they'd have more than $100,000 in positive cash flow each year. If they only wholesaled one house a month, the total profits from rentals and wholesaling more than replaced Roger's income from Alliant. If they upped that to just two homes a month, they would be able to increase that cash flow considerably—five years' time yielded over $350,000 in income for the company, and she hadn't even had the courage to estimate how big it could be if they added in two soft rehabs each year.

She'd spent the afternoon running all sorts of simulations in an Excel spreadsheet, and even though she knew all her data was based on assumptions, the numbers—in this case, a *lot* of numbers—didn't lie. Real estate investment, as John Gerber had laid it all out for them, was scalable and lucrative.

She'd also been online that afternoon, and there were people in every major town in the United States doing it. She hadn't looked, but she was willing to bet the Canadians had some version of this stuff too.

"Roger, I've got a ton of stuff to tell you, but most importantly, I think you and I need to talk to Brent and Chris about what we're doing."

He noted the way she had simply decided they would be moving into real estate investment and also the confidence that fairly oozed from the woman. It had been like this with the HELOC and the financial victory she'd won yesterday too. He had to smile. The demure woman he'd been married to for so many years had never been a shrinking violet, but he was watching Susan come back out of her shell with the ideas that they were exploring.

No … no, that wasn't it. They were not *exploring* it; they were actively *developing* it. It certainly seemed like Susan was going to do this no matter if he came along or not, but the way things were at Alliant, it certainly seemed like he had better be figuring out something to do when this house of cards that was his current career collapsed.

"Roger, honey, dinner's almost ready, but after that, let's have a talk with the boys. Can we do that tonight?"

"Yes ma'am. I think that's a great idea. Let me take off this tie and put down my briefcase first. I'm starving, so that sounds perfect."

CHAPTER TWENTY-TWO

> *Judge your success by what you had to give up in order to get it.*
>
> —Dalai Lama

Dinner had been good, as always. Susan had begun cooking more one-pot meals in August when they were financially challenged, but now in the back half of November, she had decided that hearty and wholesome was to be the order of the day.

She figured since she was now working, she would need to make a few concessions to this real estate business. In any case, her boys came first, so she would always make sure Roger and the twins got a great dinner.

Now, with the plates cleared away, the look on the twins' faces expressed they weren't sure if they were in trouble or if some sort of bad news was going to be conveyed to them.

Roger started off.

"Boys, your mother and I need to talk to you about something. It's become very important, but it also reflects a huge change in the way that we live. Especially when it comes to how your mother and I—" he struggled—"make a living."

Brent and Chris looked on, unsure of what was coming next.

"Mom and I are going to begin to invest in real estate. You've met Mr. and Mrs. Gerber next door? Well, that's what they do. They buy homes, restore them, and then sell them, or sometimes, they rent them to other people—families like us—that otherwise couldn't afford to buy their own home. Sometimes the Gerbers sell that house to that family, sometimes that family only wants to rent it, but that's how the Gerbers make a living."

Brent spoke up first, "So, Mr. Gerber doesn't work in an office like you?"

"No, Brent, he doesn't. He actually works from home, but he has some people who work for him that do have offices. I guess John could go there if he needed to, but I think most of his work is done from home."

Chris popped off next with a "cool! So, he can just work in his pajamas if he wants to?"

He smiled at the idea of a real estate tycoon in his pajamas, but he tried not to laugh. "Yes, Chris, I guess he could if he wanted to. Look, here's the important part: Over these last few months, your mom and I have had some real struggles. My company is having some really tough times, and that's made Mom and me rethink some of the things that we've always thought were right—at least when it comes to money. Some of those things you've picked up already. Like the idea of using a credit card to buy dinner. Have you seen us doing that lately?"

Chris raised his hand like a student in class. "Nope! Mom only uses her debit card now. When she said to get lunch money out of her purse one night, just like always, I saw where all the credit cards she had in her wallet were gone. She said she'd put them away, whatever that means."

Susan smiled. "Correct. And what did I tell you about that, Chris?"

The young man shot a glance at his twin brother, puffed out his chest, and said, "Credit cards are only for investments."

"That's right, son. Very good." Chris' chest puffed out further. Brent looked at him with obvious displeasure at having not answered the question and curried favor with his mother.

"I knew that too!" said Brent. "You said the same thing when we stopped for gas the other day!"

Roger knew where this was descending to, so he jumped in. "The point is this, boys. We're changing, and how we live is changing. Things that you might see your friends' parents doing aren't the things that we'll be doing or how we'll be doing it."

The conversation and the preteen questions kept up for another half-hour. Was Roger going to work for a company like Century 21? Would he be buying an SUV because all real estate agents drove SUVs? Was he going to have his name on signs in people's yards? Would he have to wear the ugly jacket like Mr. Johnson? He has to wear that weird plaid jacket his company makes him wear! Roger patiently re-explained the process, and the second time around, Brent and Chris seemed to grasp it.

Brent had a conspiratorial look on his face, and Roger, knowing his son, called him out on it. "What is it? You've got something in there. Spit it out, Brent."

"Well, Dad, I think this is really cool. But I know where the first house you need to buy is."

Brent looked at Chris and said, "Remember that one on the way to school? Past where Joseph lives? That thing is nasty—nobody's living there or taking care of it."

Chris shook his head vigorously. "Yeah! And what about the one in the neighborhood behind the school? There's that blue one where the grass is always long! Tyler caught a snake in their yard."

The boys quickly turned Roger and Susan's real estate plans into an ugliest-house contest by the time they were excused to go do their chores. Roger smiled at Susan and winked. Their kids got the picture. Susan noted Roger had asked Brent and Chris to clarify where exactly those ugly houses were located and began to note the directions.

CHAPTER TWENTY-THREE

If you want to go somewhere, it is best to find someone who has already been there.

—Robert Kiyosaki

Thursday evening found Susan and Roger neatly attired and driving to meet Louis Neiman at Canoe. While they had eaten there before, it had been some time ago. When they arrived and gave the hostess Neiman's name, she ushered them quickly to a table in the far corner past the holiday decorations and looking out over the back patio of the restaurant.

Louis Neiman stood to greet them.

"Mr. and Mrs. Alcott, obviously, I'm Louis Neiman. Welcome to dinner! I'm so pleased to meet you."

Susan shook hands demurely, and Roger was impressed by the man's hearty and firm handshake. He hadn't known what to think when Susan described her call with Neiman earlier that week, but he had assumed—wrongly—that a man in his mid-seventies might be somehow weaker. That was just the beginning of the surprises that evening.

Neiman was nursing a glass of red wine, and nearly as soon as Roger and Susan were seated, the server, who smiled and told them her name was Amethyst, swooped in to fill their water glasses and offer them a glass from the bottle Neiman had on the table.

Louis Neiman proved to be quite an enigma. To Roger, he looked like a retired schoolteacher, right down to the tweed coat he had draped over the back of his chair.

They made the obligatory small talk that newly introduced people make at dinner parties, and then Roger, always a salesman, saw that part of the conversation was at a natural lull. He decided to steer the subject.

"Mr. Neiman, I guess what I'd like to know is what drove you into the real estate investment strategy? You're obviously a well-rounded man, so to me, that suggests any number of alternate strategies in life. Why residential real estate?"

"Roger, you're in sales, aren't you?"

"Well, yes, sir. I have been my whole career."

"Please allow me to be frank but not insulting. I'm starving. Would you mind if we ate and simply had a conversation at dinner? I'm fascinated by you and your wife's story. Amethyst waits on me every week when I dine here, and she's no stranger to my eccentricities."

Roger, far from being put off, laughed. Here was a man who liked stability. He didn't want to build rapport—he wanted to observe. If he and Susan passed the test, Louis Neiman would open up to them and share. If they didn't pass, he wouldn't, and no ill would come from it. Roger felt like he had just been invited to meet a new girlfriend's parents.

"Yes sir, Mr. Neiman. I've been accused of forgetting the social part of socializing. Please forgive me."

Neiman laughed. "Roger, again, please call me Louis. My *dad* was Mr. Neiman."

Amethyst returned in a few minutes and took their order, and the meal, as always, had been exceptional. Finally, after dinner, Susan got up the nerve to start steering the conversation. "Louis, can I ask you a question? As I told you on the phone, Roger and I are getting started in real estate investment. We've talked to many people about their business models, as you know, but what I'd really like to know is what is your story? I know you've told me you were selling the last of your investment properties, but what caused you to decide to buy and sell homes outside of the classic seller agent model?"

"I guess there's no short answer to your question, Susan. I actually retired from the Georgia public school system nearly two decades ago. Now, that was a few years short of my goals, but life has a way of catching up with you. My wife, Jesse, was the picture of health in April of that year and had been involved in a minor car wreck. Since she'd had some of the symptoms of whiplash, our doctor recommended her to a specialist. In a nutshell, the MRI revealed a massive brain tumor. One that was inoperable."

Louis Neiman's eyes were focused on a place very far away as he continued, "I buried her before school started that next fall."

Suddenly, he seemed to snap back from that fall two decades ago, and his entire demeanor changed. "She was a wonderful woman, an educator like me, and the thought of going through the school year—something we had shared and laughed about year after year—was too much to bear. I had the luxury of a limited retirement, as well as her life insurance policy, so I decided to take the year off.

"I decided I needed to learn to live without her, but since teachers bring so many things home—and teachers who are married do that even more than you can imagine—the idea of sitting there at my dining room table grading papers at 9:30 at night with no one to laugh with seemed too daunting.

"I cast around for a few years, trying different things until a friend of mine, a retired surgeon I used to shoot trap with, suggested I think about investing in a rental property. He had seven homes on the east side of Atlanta that were each returning a nice cash flow, and of course, he had paid a song for them and had no debt on them.

"I've been doing that for the last seventeen years."

Roger couldn't help but see the similarities between Louis Neiman's story and John Gerber's—both men had experienced dramatic wake up calls while at the height of their previous careers and both had found ... wealth? freedom? release? ... in real estate investment.

The small voice in his head reminded Roger he was at that same stage in his career. Would it take losing his wife or his family to get his mind straight enough to make such a change?

Susan's voice brought him back to the table. "So, Louis, when you made the decision to become involved in real estate, how did you do it? Were you flipping houses? Buying rentals? How'd you learn?"

Louis smiled. "Well, Susan, today, they call it wholesaling if you do it or birddogging if you do the work for someone else. I started out looking for properties for my surgeon friend and he was, unbeknownst to me, assigning the contract. Collectively, we call that wholesaling, but it was rarely seen in the nineties. Johnny—my friend—would pay me a flat fee if I found a house that he could buy. Within just a few months, he asked me to do some of the due diligence on any potential purchase, and then, he taught me how to structure the sales contract and several other things.

"Despite me being a teacher, I couldn't see that he was mentoring me in a classically Socratic method. He'd ask me a question that he knew the answer to and then let me find the rationale for why that was the right way to do things. This was long before Google of course, so there I'd be with my Aero Atlas, my backpack phone plugged into the cigarette lighter of my sensible Buick, and my legal pad, taking notes and driving all over the east side from Decatur to Conyers doing a lot of legwork."

The money had been great, but Louis' real joy had come from creating new memories. Jesse's death had affected him deeply, and not being in a classroom became therapy for the man.

Within six months, he had helped Johnny build up his own portfolio to twelve homes, and Louis had found those properties and assigned John the contract. He'd bought his first property eight months after he'd started working with Johnny, and the man had shown him exactly how the process worked. The first full year he was investing in real estate, he replaced his teacher's salary, the second year, he doubled it.

The year he turned sixty was also the year Louis Neiman became a millionaire.

"As I look back on it, I've bought and sold—wholesaled, if you'd like—about two hundred homes."

Roger did some quick math and realized the profit on that could be well in excess of two million dollars.

"Along the way, I've kept a variety of them, some to provide owner-financing to my tenants, some as long-term rentals. Heck, today, I even do Airbnb for a couple condos I own in Buckhead. I've decided that as much as I love it, I'd like to turn the page on this career.

"In the last year, I've sold most of the higher end properties I own—the nice houses in nice neighborhoods—and I've been slowly liquidating the rest of the homes in my portfolio."

"What are your plans, Louis? Where are you going if you leave real estate?" asked Roger.

"I decided to move to a lovely home I had rebuilt outside of Sarasota, Florida. I've always loved the west coast of Florida, and there's enough golf and fishing there to last me all the time I have left.

"Aside from the two condos, I have a total of twenty-three homes still in my portfolio. Eleven are in one subdivision in Conyers, and the rest are in Dekalb County. Now that we've shared some conversation, I'd like to sell them all at once."

Louis Neiman looked Roger dead in the eye. "And I'd like to sell them to you."

Roger, used to being the closer, didn't see that he'd just been closed. His body went stiff, he folded his arms, and as a salesman, he knew that whoever spoke next was going to lose. He couldn't help himself as he opened his mouth, "Well, Louis … I … we …"

"Roger, I understand. You can't say yes right now. You don't know anything about the properties; you don't even know what I'm asking for them. There are a hundred objections, and honestly, you don't even know enough about the business to know what they are.

"I've prepared a portfolio for you to review and follow up with me. Undoubtedly, you're thinking, *Why?* and here's the reason: My home is going to be ready for me to move into in February, and I'm actually flying out to Lake Tahoe to spend Christmas with my cousin and his family. I'll be gone until about January 15, but I can certainly make myself available for any calls you or your mentors might have. In a pinch, I can jump on a Skype call to talk about anything you might wish."

Louis Neiman raised his hand at Amethyst and made a motion with his hand. A moment later, the young lady brought a large file folder over to the table. In it were detailed photos of all the properties Louis wanted to sell and nearly fifty pages of material.

"Roger, Susan, this is what I'm going to sell. Take it, look at it, do your research. When—and if—you would like to discuss buying these, we'll have a call to discuss the pricing and the financing on it.

"No doubt, you are both thinking, *This old man has gone off his rocker*, and perhaps I have. I could likely make another small fortune if I listed these all separately, but I can't spend what I have now. Why not put it to a better use? *That's* why I wanted to meet with you tonight. I wanted to see if you were people who would do *something* with it, not just turn it into a paycheck. I get the impression that you two—and your sons—might take this opportunity to make a better life—to recapture the American dream, to create generational wealth."

Susan's smile beamed. "Louis, I don't know what to say."

He looked at them both. "Perhaps I can unchain one more elephant before I leave this earth."

Roger looked at Susan, and Susan looked at Roger, and then they both looked at Louis. In chorus, they both repeated, "Unchain one more elephant?"

Neiman laughed. "Yes, exactly! In India, of course, the elephant is a beast of burden. How can you possibly control such a creature? It's got the strength of hundreds of men. It's simple—when the elephant is still an infant, its captors, or owners as it were, chain it to a sturdy tree. As it grows, the elephant has learned it cannot break the chain that binds it to the tree. As a mature animal, the poor creature still doesn't understand that it possesses all the strength it could possibly need to simply walk away. In short, it quit testing its own strength against either the chain or the tree.

"Many times, that creature will never be able to grasp it was strong enough to walk away anytime. Perhaps I can help you both to see that the chains that bind you to the middle class are only in your mind."

With that, Louis Neiman shook Roger's hand, kissed Susan's hand, and the three of them walked out of the restaurant and into the parking lot.

CHAPTER TWENTY-FOUR

Everything you want is on the other side of fear.

—Jack Canfield

As late as it was when Roger and Susan returned home that evening, they spent time looking through every property that Louis had included in his portfolio. The same information appeared on each page—the age of the house, the age of the various systems in the house—furnace, air conditioner, roof, water heater—and, surprisingly, how long Neiman had owned it, the cash flow figures, rents, and maintenance budgets and estimated expenses for the fiscal year.

Susan recognized the paperwork as something custom that Neiman had to have had designed, but she reasoned (correctly, she later learned) that it made the bookkeeping and taxes easier. She made a mental note that she and Roger would need just such a system at some point.

It was after one o'clock the next morning when they went to bed, and both husband and wife slept soundly.

When he got home from work Friday afternoon, Roger immediately took the portfolio to John Gerber, but Patricia told him that John was gone for the night to Asheville to speak at a seminar. He thanked her and asked if it would be okay if he interrupted their Sunday with some questions for John.

Patricia had laughed aloud and said she'd planned on John being home by one o'clock, and dinner would be at six, so anytime Roger wanted to sneak over in the interim was fine.

When they got up Saturday morning, Roger decided that he and Susan would go look at houses. The boys were going to a Christmas party that day, so their parents had a few hours to burn. Roger and Susan jumped into the Lexus like escaping prisoners and pointed the car toward Gwinnett County, their neighbor to the east.

Three hours later, they had a list of run down, unoccupied homes they felt *must* be able to be bought inexpensively, so they picked up the twins and began playing around on the local tax commissioner's website.

They quickly pared down their list of thirty-one homes to thirteen as they cross-referenced images from Google Earth and the tax records. By the time the family decided to go out to a local Mexican restaurant for dinner, Roger was cautiously optimistic that this could be the beginning of their real estate business.

At three o'clock Sunday afternoon, Roger knocked on John Gerber's back door, and John answered it.

"Roger! Patricia said you'd come by. How are you?"

"John, I'm great, but I've got a ton of questions I'm not even sure how to answer, or even where to start."

"I see. Well, come in out of the cold and let's talk about it all."

The men sat down in the living room, and Roger sat down with Louis Neiman's file and the legal pad with each of the thirteen homes he and Susan had found the day before. Gerber looked at them, but didn't pick them up, imagining the other man was going to get to those in due time. Roger jumped right in, explaining that he and Susan had met Louis Neiman for dinner two nights before and that Neiman had made a veiled offer for his remaining homes.

Gerber nodded along, asking for clarification on certain points of the discussion but saying nothing.

Roger then moved on toward how he and Susan had gone riding the day before and tracked down homes that seemed to be in a shape which suggested their owners would be inclined to sell inexpensively. Finally, he turned the Neiman file and the legal pad of notes around for Gerber to look at.

At first, the man did nothing.

After a pregnant pause, he began to talk. He did, in fact, know Louis Neiman personally. He'd never done business with the man, but his reputation had always been impeccable.

"Roger, I don't know a soul in the Atlanta market who dislikes him. He's helped a lot of people in our business, but he's also helped hundreds, hell, *thousands*, of people to find a fairly priced place to live. He's up-front, honest to a fault, and even when he's had to evict tenants, he's done so in such a professional manner that even the tenants can't get pissed about it.

"You might say," John continued, "he doesn't deal in absolutes like profit and loss but in what he feels is morally right and wrong. Despite the fact that these homes could easily be sold to other investors, I've been aware of his desire to sell these last two dozen or so to a new investor for about six months.

"The fact that you made it through dinner and actually got to see the file of the properties tells me he likes what you had to say. He'd never simply sell them to the highest bidder. In fact, I'd guess that if you agreed to buy them that night, he'd have said no."

"Why?" asked Roger.

"Louis is a teacher. He's helped a lot of men and women get their start in real estate in this area. Yesterday, in Asheville, I even met someone who had been mentored by Louis. He loves to give back."

Prompted by the comment about Asheville, Roger changed the subject. "Speaking of that, what were you doing there?"

"Learning, Roger, learning. As an entrepreneur, all too often we're the smartest people in an empty room. You have to keep learning, and you have to find groups, or symposiums, or seminars, or something to keep your mind sharp, to introduce new ideas, or to find new ways to operate the systems in your business. You do it at Alliant on the company dime, and I do it at JG Limited on my dime, although I do write it off on my taxes."

"So, there are places to go to *learn* this stuff?"

"Of course! Any given weekend, seasoned investors are sharing ways to invest in single family real estate, there are webinars every day from different thought leaders, and personal training is available from mentors all over.

"I was asked to speak in Asheville because one of my old students is about to release a new book, so he asked me to give the keynote at his training event. Enough of that—let's look at your list."

Roger scooted over as John pulled out his iPad and began typing in addresses and telling Roger what he thought of the properties.

Ninety minutes later, Roger was pleased that each of the thirteen properties had made John's cut. Gerber had looked at his watch, scowled, and shared with Roger several things he and Susan would need to do next.

"You'll need to call and talk to buyers about what exactly they are looking for. We're all quite different in our standards."

Roger flipped open his legal pad to the list he had made and asked Gerber about the eight investors on it. Gerber recognized them all and explained which of the properties Roger and Susan had identified made sense to explore with each of the investors.

Finally, at the top of the hour, Roger realized that he had monopolized Gerber's afternoon. He apologized as he packed up the files and his notes, and Gerber smiled. "Roger, don't worry about it. I'm happy to act as a mentor for you and Susan. If you can wholesale any of these homes, you can make money. More importantly, though, you need to really get under Louis' offer. I know you said he's out of town for the holidays but reach out to him this week—no—*tomorrow*—and tell him you'd like to know more. You can use my name—I don't think Louis will mind—and see what the actual offer is. Something this big takes some time to understand, but you've still got a few months."

Roger's face bunched up. "What?"

Gerber smiled and indicated the calendar on the wall by the back door. "You started exploring what was out there about six months ago. You've gone through your *Four Entrepreneurial Freedoms*, you are starting to understand my ideas of Deals, Money, and People, and I told you I thought you could make this change—if you wanted to—in less than nine months.

"You got a clear understanding of the fundamentals to make this leap, so in the next three months, you could have everything you wanted ... *if* you want it."

Roger shook Gerber's outstretched hand. "I do. Thanks, John."

CHAPTER TWENTY-FIVE

Amateurs sit and wait for inspiration, the
rest of us just get up and go to work.

—Stephen King

Roger and Susan learned a few things in the next two weeks. The first was that no one seemed inclined to return calls around Christmas. County offices, banks, and even some of the investors they reached out to all seemed to have dropped everything for the holidays.

Susan could understand investors and entrepreneurs—they had made their money; they could spend time and the holidays any way they choose. On the other hand, county workers, municipal clerks? It was frustrating.

If the week before Christmas was aggravating, the week after Christmas was excruciating.

Roger understood—it had always been a pain in the ass to get people to accomplish anything in the last few weeks of the year. Some were on vacation, and the budgets for the quarter—and thus the year—were shot and spent, so no one wanted to spend any money unless they absolutely had to, and most didn't.

They made some headway on Louis' properties. They had gone and driven by each of them as a family. They had budgeted out Christmas, a first in the Alcott home, but everyone was getting exactly what they wanted, and Roger and Susan had paid cash for the entire thing. Susan and Louis had exchanged emails multiple times, and Roger, Susan, and Louis had had a Skype call earlier that week. Roger noted it was snowing in Tahoe in the picture window behind Louis on the video call.

Neiman was pleased they would like to move forward and told them he would have the rest of the information—including the offer and the terms—FedEx'd on January 3. Roger opened his mouth to ask why, but Louis anticipated the question.

"Roger, you still have to deal with a company that is dying, and you have kids. Our business is not so big as to demand your attention when you can celebrate the birth of Christ with your family. Why do you think I'm out here?"

Roger smiled because he knew this, and he knew himself. *Higher Purpose, right, Rog?* said the voice in his head. "Yes, sir."

Thus, the Christmas holidays passed without any more fanfare—and less stress—than any other year. When Roger and his family gathered in the living room on New Year's Eve to watch the ball drop in Times Square, he had a sense of optimism that he couldn't recall from years past. Right or wrong, the New Year would bring change to the Alcott household.

* * * *

His own sales experience had long ago told him that every sales call was different, and he should expect certain things based on what most sales experts considered the *warmth* of the call. A true cold call—just knocking on a door or making a phone call—might yield a closing ratio of one in every hundred.

A call that was lukewarm might yield a ratio of one in twenty, depending on the product you were selling.

A hot call might close every other time.

Nothing prepared him or Susan for the challenges that their list presented them. One by one, they had made contact with the owners; one by one, they had been told no or even, in one case, cursed at and hung up on. Susan, ever the optimist, figured that every call added to their experience, and when Roger spied John in the backyard one Saturday afternoon, he asked him about it.

"John, this is a lot more frustrating than I ever thought."

"Well, now just think about it, Roger. You've interjected yourself into these people's lives, and even if they entertained you, they would undoubtedly be insulted by a price. No offense, but are you even confident in how to make an offer?"

Alcott stopped and thought about it. "Well, actually, John, maybe I'm not. I mean, none of these calls has even gotten to that phase."

"And that's usually how it goes. Your chances of getting a motivated seller by finding an ugly house is very small, in my experience. I didn't make that clear a few weeks ago, because quite frankly, I wasn't sure what you'd planned to do with that list. This is the primary reason we use bandit signs. The people that call us are *motivated* sellers."

Roger chewed on the inside of his lip for a minute and then asked, "Why would anyone with a house that is visibly deteriorating *not* be motivated to sell it?"

"Oh, let me count the ways ... Some live in the fantasy that they'll be the ones to start fixing it up to rent—they're just waiting on something—cash, a tenant, a winning lottery ticket, you name it. Others would never sell it because it was a family home, and they can't bear to let it go, and to them, it's somehow easier to let it rot under their lack of care than it is to let someone else rehab it and make it into something better than they could. Still others—especially in areas like Atlanta—think that any piece of real estate in this city is made of gold. The old real estate investment adage about property, 'They aren't making any more of it,' is true, but not to the extent that some people would believe. I won't buy a home to rent in a neighborhood that I wouldn't let my wife drive in, so no matter how good a deal is in a terrible part of town, I won't waste time on it. I know there are deals to be had there, but if I don't feel safe, how can I expect someone else to?

"There's one more thing, Roger. Maybe you hadn't thought about it, maybe you had, but you have to acknowledge it. Any list you have of houses, buyers, sellers, *anything,* is going to have to be cared for. You won't make money with a list of ten houses unless you're constantly adding to that list.

"Is that so different from the lists you would keep at Alliant? If one carrier can't make a load, do you just let that load sit on the dock? Well, do you?"

Roger shook his head, and John continued.

"Exactly. That's the key—one goes down, and three more replace it. You can understand metrics, so you'll understand that you might go thirty homes before you close one, then BOOM! You close four in a row. Real estate, if you do it this way, is just a numbers game. You can't chase bumblebees, but you have to vet every one of those bumblebees before you let them go.

"I'll tell you what. We've got a few minutes—let's go for a ride."

He walked over to the door leading to the garage and grabbed a set of keys off of a hook. He looked over his shoulder at Roger. "You coming?"

Moments later, Roger found himself sitting in the Town Car. It was older but immaculate. He looked over at the dashboard—the odometer read 38,765 miles. "John, I've got to ask—where'd you get this car? I mean, I know you pay cash, but …"

"But you'd think I could afford a flashier car?" said Gerber, laughing.

Roger blushed but had to be honest. "Well, I guess so. But well, that sounds so … crass. I'm sorry. I shouldn't have said it."

He laughed the hearty laugh of a happy man. "Actually, Roger, I drive Lincolns for a couple of different reasons. One, my father. He always thought they were the cat's meow but could never afford one.

In fact, the only time I'm sure the man rode in one was to his funeral, and I'm the one who made sure of that.

"The second reason is that Lincoln built about a gazillion of this model, and every old fart in the nation bought them and then died without having ever driven the damn things over forty-five miles an hour. I buy one of these low mileage puppies every two years when someone has put another fossil in a nursing home, put about fifty or sixty thousand miles on them, and sell them for what I paid for them. Best deal in the car business."

Roger nodded.

"The last reason is really the business reason. They look professional but not pretentious. When I go to meet a seller, they see an older car and an older man. They don't get caught up in how much money I've spent on a Cadillac or a big Diesel truck. It makes the offer I'm going to make them look more *real*."

Roger made a mental note as he reflected on his Lexus and Susan's Range Rover. She'd been talking about trading down for a less expensive vehicle for months now, but he'd never really given it too much thought.

The gleaming Town Car turned left at the end of the block when Roger expected to turn right. He looked over at John. "Where are we going?"

"Oh, just around the neighborhood."

Roger was confused. "Why, John? I mean, we were just talking about buying houses."

"Yes, we were. And buying houses from motivated sellers, right?"

Roger nodded and Gerber continued, "Then, we'd better find some motivated sellers if you're going to buy anything and keep your shirt."

As Roger was opening his mouth to ask him why they were riding around in their own neighborhood to discuss finding houses inexpensively, Gerber indicated the house they were passing.

"*That* one. Charlene Jones and her husband, Thomas, own it. Charlene just left Thomas and emptied out their bank accounts doing it. They needed two incomes to pay for it, along with the two cars they have financed. The good news is that Thomas hates the house and has to move. He's paid nearly ten years on a fifteen-year mortgage on it and has about $300,000 in equity in it. Unfortunately, as close as he is to paying it off, he just wants out. Too many bad memories. You could probably buy it for $240,000 cash—and that includes paying off the rest of the note. I'd expect you could assign that contract and make a quick fifteen grand on it inside of two weeks."

Roger looked at John in disbelief. The Lincoln continued driving on deeper into the neighborhood.

Two right turns later, and the Town Car glided into a cul-de-sac. Gerber indicated a regal-looking, if somewhat dated, brick two-story home with a yard that was obviously attended to by someone with more pressing things to do.

"Maxine Carter, age sixty-eight, a widow. She owns this house free and clear. She paid it off after her husband passed away seven years ago. Unfortunately, Maxine's children have moved away from the area, and she relies on the kid next door to handle the yard. If you look closely, the roof is at its operating limit—those are the original shingles, and the air conditioner is about sixteen years old. There's also the question of drainage on the lot. The French drain the builder was supposed to have placed to sluice storm water off is either clogged or half-assed, so Maxine routinely gets water—or at least moisture—in her basement. The house is a hair over twenty-four years old and probably needs to be gutted and rethought to make it sellable today."

Roger looked at the home, then looked back at John. "Why wouldn't you simply do a soft rehab on it and rent it?"

"Who wants to live in a gated community in a crappy house?" John asked. That's like putting shiny rims on a car that burns oil and runs poorly. The tenants you could attract at that price-point lower the home values in a neighborhood like this. Sooner or later, the HOA will make her clean it up, but she's ready to move to Sun City down in Hilton Head and start acting her age."

Roger rubbed his chin in deep thought as John went on.

"This is a clear example of what I'd consider a gut job. With the roof and the A/C replacement costs, you're already into five figures, and you haven't addressed what are undoubtedly ugly bathrooms and a dated kitchen. This is a wholesale deal."

John looked over at Roger. "You could buy that one for $140,000 cash and, again, assigning the contract to an investor who'd likely be comfortable buying at a hundred fifty grand and prepared to put up another fifty or seventy-five to really do it right."

And on they went through the neighborhood. John pointed out several other homes he seemed to know details of that no mere neighborhood gossip could have told him. As they pulled back onto their own street, Roger finally asked the question that had been burning in his mind since the first house.

"John, how do you know all this?"

Gerber smiled and said simply, "Two actually were from signs, but one came from a referral from a direct mail piece we sent out. Even though I don't mail in our neighborhood, Thomas Jones' mother received a mailer two weeks ago and set it aside for her son. No matter how, each one of these people—far from my target seller—has reached out to my team to discuss selling their home. That's the other thing about driving a common car—nobody worries about what *you're* doing. The neighbors see it and figure an old friend has stopped by."

Roger nodded. "So, you don't even have a magnetic sign you stick on your car? There's a guy in town who has his car all lettered up—logo, phone numbers, website. You don't do that?"

"I have, but the downside is that in a lot of neighborhoods, the people selling the house don't want to put their business out there for everyone to see. At the same time, if you make an offer on a house—say, $55,000—and they don't take it immediately—and most don't—now the guy next door has seen your car and walks over to be nosy. He offers them $70,000 because he's an idiot, or he convinces them not to sell. I just don't care for the stuff on the car, but it can be very effective. As a matter of fact, I have an old friend in Virginia who more than paid for the Escalade he drives by lettering it."

As they pulled up in the driveway, John looked at Roger and said, "Do you see how the marketing works for you? I've got a sheet I can email you tonight—it's basically everything you need to ask for when someone calls you. In the good old days, I used it personally to keep me on task when a seller called, but now the answering service we contract with uses it to handle all of our direct mail responses. The idea is simple: before you jump in the car or waste any time, you need to know if the deal has any legs. Anything else is wasted effort."

CHAPTER TWENTY-SIX

*Without ambition one starts nothing. Without
work one finishes nothing. The prize will
not be sent to you. You have to win it.*

—Ralph Waldo Emerson

Lake Tahoe was snowed in on January 3, and it was late in the afternoon of the fifth before FedEx could pick up the contract and a *Letter of Intent* that Louis Neiman had drafted for Roger and Susan to execute.

Nonetheless, the FedEx man dutifully brought an overnight mailer to the Alcotts' door late on the evening of January 6. Roger was on his way home, and rather than open it without him, Susan signed for the package and waited for her husband to arrive.

Well, Louis certainly sent something, Susan thought. The damned thing must have weighed nearly three pounds!

Once Roger was home and had greeted his family, Susan brought in the package. "Do we dare open it now, or should we wait until after dinner?"

"Susan, I think you know if we open that now, there won't be a dinner." Roger laughed.

She agreed, so the family sat down and shared how their respective days had gone. The twins reported that all their friends had nice Christmases and joked that everyone's mother must have bought new clothes from the same rack because many of the kids at school were wearing the same styles and colors.

Roger shared that Alliant was expecting to report catastrophic losses and the reorganization when the quarterly reports were issued, and it appeared the annual report, due out two weeks after that, would indicate a company that was struggling but trying to recover.

Susan related some of her progress she'd made for the real estate company, and that this was the week she planned to file all the LLC paperwork with the Secretary of State website. She'd been researching the process half-heartedly over the holidays but had hit a wall with taking care of the boys, handling the due diligence on Louis' properties, and honestly, the holiday season, in general.

"The good news, though, is that we can do it all online. In fact—here's a fun fact—there's some pretty inexpensive software we can buy to send out invoices and pay them. If we have renters, we can even automate their rent payments. It's 'set it and forget it' like that crummy oven they used to advertise on infomercials."

Roger sat back and thought about how different he felt about life now. If this same sort of deal had been FedEx'd to him a year ago, he'd have grabbed it and disappeared for the night. He might still have done it if it was Alliant, although every week, he felt himself growing past that. The hard charger he had been was slowly softening into a man with radically different priorities.

Finally, Chris asked to be excused, and that was when Roger and Susan got up to go open Louis Neiman's offer.

* * * *

And it was a sweet one. Louis would sell his entire portfolio—except the two condos he owned in Buckhead—for $1.3 million with 10% down at closing. He had a provision to extend financing to the Alcotts if they decided to do so, and the paperwork with the offer included how Louis and the Alcotts could avoid cross-collateralizing the assets if the Alcotts sought to sell some of the properties at a later date with some debt still owed.

Roger did find it interesting to see, in the hand-written note that Louis had included as a cover page, that Louis truly hoped Roger and Susan would consider this, as he wanted to leave a legacy to somebody who would take his own hard work and continue to grow it.

To Roger, it sounded more like the language of a father bequeathing an inheritance than a sales letter.

Finally, there was the financing. Again, Louis had alluded to it in the letter, stating it was a ten-year package, "… if I live that long."

Roger and Susan took a long time to work through the entire contents of the package that evening. Neiman had included cash flow projections, pro-formas on each home in the portfolio, as well as a list of previous expenditures, such as roofs, water heaters, and air conditioning units. Some of the material was a duplicate of the information Louis had shared in the original portfolio, but most of it was new, or at least formatted in a different manner. To Susan, ever the bookkeeper, the inclusion of a depreciation schedule on the homes allowed her to see that either cash or accrual accounting could be used for their company.

Finally, at nearly midnight, they pushed away from the dining room table and decided to call it a night.

"What do you think, honey?" she asked.

Roger shook his head. "God knows there's a lot of stuff here, maybe even too much. I mean, he's documenting things that we've never even thought about. Until I Googled *cross collateralization*, I'd never even heard of it. Honestly, it scares me. I mean, I know we can handle it, but can we sleep at night knowing how far out we're extended financially? Maybe if I stayed at Alliant for another year, I would feel okay about it."

Susan scowled at her husband's statement. "Roger Jonathan Alcott, what's the point of doing all this if you have to stay in *that* dumpster fire? I want to do this with you, not by myself."

"I know, I know," Roger said, cutting off his wife. "I just worry if I—*we* can handle that kind of leverage and stress. I mean, just the note on the debt is going to be over ten grand a month. I know the business is profitable, but is there enough in it to provide us—all of us—with the quality of life we've come to expect?"

Susan smiled at Roger. "Well, you know what? We can *make* it profitable." And with that, she turned and went upstairs to get ready for bed.

Roger looked out into the night at where he knew John Gerber's home lay in the darkness. Gerber would know what to do. Gerber could tell him what to do. Tomorrow, he'd go and ask John about this whole thing.

* * * *

"I don't know, Roger," said John when the two men stood in Gerber's kitchen the next day as Roger filled Gerber in on the blanks of Neiman's offer. "For me, personally, it's a perfect deal, and I've done a lot worse."

Roger, still nervous about the amount of debt this required and his own lack of knowledge of the business, decided to call the only lifeline he could think of. "John, would you consider partnering with us on this deal?"

John smiled. "Roger, absolutely not. Being a mentor is one thing, but being a partner is a lot harder. You know, 'Good fences making good neighbors' and all that drivel. Besides, Louis would undoubtedly rescind his offer if I was involved. Nothing personal, but I think Louis has taken a shine to you guys and wants to share the freedom that he's learned how to create in his life with someone else whom he sees as being trapped in the American dream."

Gerber continued, "It's my opinion—which you have paid exactly nothing to receive—that Louis would view my involvement in this deal exactly as it is—you wanting a crutch, not a commitment. Louis intends to sell these properties to someone who can commit .to changing themselves and their lives."

Roger, caught in his own insecurities, blushed at what he suddenly realized was the truth.

Seeing Roger suddenly get it, John pressed his point. "Roger, do you want to do this or not? If you do, you'll have an incredible opportunity from a man who has more integrity in his finger than many people have in their lives. If Louis Neiman has a flaw, it's seeing the world as he wants it to be, not as it is. For him, the skies are always going to be blue, and the clouds will always be white. He's the embodiment of the Louis Armstrong song, 'What a Wonderful World.'"

John seemed to move a bit closer to Roger. "In other words, are you a wantrepreneur or an entrepreneur?"

Gerber sat down heavily at the table and motioned for Roger to do the same. "I can't make up your mind for you. I can't peer into a crystal ball and tell you everything is going to be perfect. I *can* tell you that if you don't do this deal, you will lose something, something you've gained these last few months. You'll have made a decision to simply be a company man, and for all that's worth, you might as well go ahead and tell your family they aren't important to you. Tell your boss that you'll happily carry his piss bucket until Alliant finally burns to the ground."

Roger snapped back. "But John—"

Gerber cut him off and stood up, "No buts. No ifs. Either do it or don't do it. Roger, I can't make you do anything, but I can demand that you make a decision. I can demand that you take responsibility. Now, I apologize for being frank, but I hear this all the time, this ... this ... silliness!"

Gerber was agitated now, standing up and very nearly flailing his arms. "If you want a sure thing, then go work for someone who had the stones to take the chance. Plug yourself back into the Matrix and forget about how things are in the real world. Go back to wondering where people are going to work and why they're smiling. Roger, please understand, where you are now is exactly where every real estate investor inevitably has to pass through. It's Milton's Slough of Despond. Go forward or go back, but you cannot stay here."

John sighed. "My advice? Talk about it with Susan, pray about it, debate about it, and do all that knowing fully that on some specific date in the very near future, you will either move forward or step away. Can you do that?"

Roger nodded his head. "Yes, I can."

John put out his hand. "Then, when you make the right decision, come tell me."

Walking back to his own home, Roger thought it strange that John hadn't said what the right decision was.

CHAPTER TWENTY-SEVEN

*Genius is one percent inspiration and
ninety-nine percent perspiration.*

—Thomas Edison

Roger and Susan knew Louis would be returning on
January 15, so they agreed they would make a decision
no later than the fourteenth. Ironically, Louis was the
one who told them not to make a decision yet.

They'd been on a Skype call with Neiman, asking
a few questions they knew wouldn't make them sound
too dumb when Neiman simply said, "I hope you
weren't planning on saying yes before I got home. I've
got some things still to share with you."

Roger and Susan had looked at one another, then
back to the computer screen, and simply agreed with
the man.

So, despite trying to take John Gerber's advice,
Roger's deadline was inadvertently pushed back. Louis

had made arrangements to have the Alcotts meet him at his office the next Saturday morning at ten o'clock. Much to their surprise, when they pulled up, they not only saw Louis Neiman's Mercedes but also four newer pickup trucks and a cargo van.

In the office stood Louis Neiman and five burly men who looked as if they could have picked up the building and carried it off. The group were laughing and carrying on, drinking coffee, and as soon as Roger and Susan walked in the door, Louis was quick to introduce them to the men.

"These are the backbone of my business—each of them has worked with me as contractors for at least ten years and is among the best you'll find."

Each of them shook hands with the Alcotts and then, as if on cue, four of them walked into the parking lot. Roger looked at Louis with a puzzled expression on his face.

Neiman, anticipating the question, said simply, "They know what we're here for, so we'll make it brief."

Over the next thirty minutes, Louis called each man into the office and asked him to share with Roger what his specialties were. Louis explained how each man charged and how he paid the man's business accounts. Finally, after all the men were gone, Susan asked, "What was that all about?"

Louis smiled and said, "I trust every one of those men implicitly, but in this business, you have to verify everything. I wanted each of them to have the chance to say or explain anything we might have going on, so that as we move forward in this sale, no one gets amnesia about how my business has been run or when each of those men and their teams get paid."

With the contractors gone, the three sat down to allow the Alcotts time to ask any questions. Susan started it off, "Louis, I guess the biggest concern I … we … have is just making sure we understand the day-to-day operations. I mean, I know how to run a bookkeeping business, and obviously Roger understands the logistics industry backwards and forwards, but we're going to have to be learning as we go."

Both men nodded in agreement at Susan's observation.

She continued, "I feel confident that within a relatively short time, we have the wherewithal to handle this—enterprise—but how do we grow it? I mean, it's obvious that you have all your ducks in a row, but in the end, we want to be able to expand."

Neiman nodded. "I understand, Susan. You're not looking to buy a job; you're looking to grow a business. I've felt that was what you and Roger were thinking since our first call. In fact, that's what drew me to you."

Again, Susan looked at Roger, but this time, Roger spoke, "Yes, Louis, I guess that's it. I've never had any challenge selling or asking people for the business. I think I understand the logic behind bandit signs, but I just don't know …" he let the sentence trail off.

Louis smiled. "I get it. Once you attract a motivated seller, there are still any number of steps you have to take to get the deal. Someone that is up against the wall to sell a house might not be, shall we say, forthright in telling you about termites, or a roof leak, or lead-based paint. All of which can bite you in the ass if you don't find that out on the front end. What you need to be able to do is to understand what we call the after-repaired value—we call it the ARV—and how much it will cost to get it there."

They both leaned closer to Neiman as he continued speaking. "Let's say someone comes to you wanting to sell you their house. They own it free and clear, but the damned thing is a mess. You'll look at the comps in the area—comparable homes that have sold recently. I like to keep my comps as close as possible geographically because subtle changes like school district or even traffic can distort a comp. Some investors like to compare the ages of homes, but I don't."

He continued, "A new home in the area is just as likely to sell as an older home, and the market in metro areas is very similar. Companies that are truly rehabbing homes for sale are competing directly against new construction, so I usually factor in any comparable home, regardless of age. Now, if you're in an older neighborhood here on the north side where it's fashionable to tear down the 1950s-era home and build new, then you really have to be careful, but let's be real—that's a very specialized example."

Susan and Roger both nodded in acknowledgment.

"So, you figure that a reasonable comp for that style of house—let's say a three-bedroom, two-bath starter—is $140,000 in your seller's neighborhood. Remember our example is a mess, so it's going to need a roof, a new air conditioner, new appliances, carpet, and a lot of love on the exterior and in the yard ..." Suddenly, the man stopped and snapped his fingers. "Damn!"

Reaching into his desk, he pulled out a laminated copy of something and held it up. "My cheat sheet. I use this to estimate repairs based on the costs that my team—the men you met today—charge. I bid it out each year to keep them honest. I'll make you a copy before you leave."

Roger and Susan looked at the sheet Neiman had just produced—here was everything they had needed—a breakdown of every conceivable cost issue to arrive at the total cost of repairing a home!

Roger was floored. "So we just document all the broken stuff in a home, subtract it from the ARV, and that's the offer?"

Neiman shook his head. "Not unless you'd like to lose your shirt. You'll take the ARV, subtract the repair costs, and then your offer will be 65 to 70 percent of that number. Remember, this is a *for-profit* business."

Nodding her head, Susan seemed to understand. "I get it—we're offering them a service, not a handout. What if they countered on that offer with something like 80 percent?"

"You have to be careful with that," said Louis. "Remember, when you own the house, it costs money to *hold* the house. Aside from the usual things like power bills and the like, you have to factor in commissions, legal costs, any challenges with the title on the property, and even the costs of a survey if the seller doesn't have a current one. If you don't have any capital costs, and you're sure you can still easily sell it, then it might be a safe bet. If you're paying for the money to use in the deal, and you're looking to keep it long term, then it is probably smarter to pass on it. Remember, these folks are *motivated*—they have to sell the house. If they don't sell it to you, they will sell it to someone. Personally, I stick to the 65-70% rule; there is always another deal out there. In the end, you're looking for fifteen to twenty percent as profit."

Neiman looked at Roger. "You're the sales expert. Do you buy the product or buy the story?"

"You're right—story sells, but yes, you have to trust and verify, like you said earlier with your contractors."

He was smiling. "Roger, Susan, what do you think is an acceptable closing ratio for buying homes in a model like this? I know John Gerber is a friend of yours and is mentoring you, but based on what you've learned, how many noes will you get before you get a yes?"

Roger and Susan looked at other again and looked back at Neiman. Roger spoke up, "Louis, I'd guess one in twenty? Maybe twenty-five? Like you said, these people are motivated, and they are the ones who started the conversation. If they truly have to sell and they are accurately representing themselves, I'd say that's a fair ratio."

"Good guess and an accurate one," said Neiman. "Now think about how much a no is worth. Actually, let me say that another way—look out the window. The next car that passes will be a red car—would you bet on that?"

"Louis, we have no way of knowing tha—" said Susan as a grey sedan drove past Neiman's office.

"Keep watching," said Louis, "but listen while you watch. If every deal you close is worth $20,000, and your closing ration is one in twenty, then every answer—yes and no—is worth $1,000."

By now, seven cars had passed—whites and greys and blacks and even a bright blue but no red cars.

Finally, after four minutes, the eighteenth car to pass Neiman's office was a bright red coupe.

"See? I assure you; you could watch all day, and the numbers—the metrics—would stay the same. There are only so many colors that a car can be painted, but the buying public doesn't buy as many red cars as they do all the other colors. In fact, only about one in twenty new cars sold are red. Your motivated seller? They're the red car."

Neiman voice lowered, and he looked stern, like the former teacher was about to give the Alcotts an exam. "*Always* make an offer if someone has asked you to come assess their home. No matter how basic it is, always leave them with a price and a way to reach you. *Never say no for the other guy.*"

He stood up from the desk, took his repair cost sheet to the other room, and photocopied it. He came back and handed the Alcotts two copies of it. "Now, Roger and Susan, if there's anything you need this week, please feel free to reach out to me. I think—I hope—we're getting close, but I'm sure there are a few things you'll still want to sort out. I have every intention of availing myself to you both for at least the first quarter you're in business. I hate to chat and run, but I've got a call with the GC handling my house in Sarasota today, and he's run into some trouble on the plumbing."

With that, the Alcotts shook hands with Neiman, thanked him again, and went out to the car.

As they drove away, Susan was the first to speak, "Roger, what do you think?"

The man kept his eyes on the road and simply said, "I don't know …" and his voice trailed off.

* * * *

Monday morning dawned cold and overcast. Roger and Susan had tiptoed around Louis' offer Sunday and finally directly addressed it late in the afternoon. Susan had come into the dining room where Roger had been looking at the local MLS on his laptop and quietly said, "Roger, what do you think?"

Roger had looked up, taken off his glasses, and looked at his wife. "I… I just…" And shook his head. "I think it's a great deal, and I can't see where we could go wrong, but I'm nervous about it. I mean, there's got to be a *gotcha* in here," he said as he pointed to the folder with Louis' offer in it. "If we buy all twenty-three houses, and we need to sell one, or a tenant makes us an offer on one, can we even sell it? I want to ask John about it, but he's out of town."

"Roger, really? You've had more than enough time to ask all the questions you could ever dream up. I've asked mine, and I'm convinced. What can I do to help you make a decision, no matter what that decision is?"

Now, Monday at 10:15 in the morning, Roger sat looking at the phone on his desk at Alliant like a man looking at a grenade. He knew the answers he needed were on the other end of the phone, and all he needed to do was pick it up, dial a few numbers, and he'd place himself in a position to make a decision.

Go ahead, Rog, said the voice in his head. Get it over with. *Make the call. You already know who you need to talk to about this deal, and you've been goofing around for weeks, looking for the excuse not to make it.*

Finally, he picked up the phone, dialed the number he had long ago memorized, and spoke to the friendly voice that answered on the first ring.

* * * *

Roger didn't hate attorneys, but he didn't like them too much either. Nonetheless, one of his college friends had come to work in Atlanta years ago and had worked long and hard to get his name on the firm's boilerplate as their resident real estate attorney.

As he navigated the midday traffic on his way to the firm's office in Buckhead, he knew this meant the last excuse for not taking Louis' offer was going to be addressed. If his old friend, Stanley, pronounced Louis' contract airtight, Roger couldn't help but take it.

Roger—*and Susan, don't forget her*—would then be on the hook for not only all the debt he already had, but he'd also be stacking another million dollars or so on top of that and inevitably having to lose the job that was currently paying for all of it.

It was a terrifying change for a man who was grounded in routine, systems, and processes.

Two hours later, Roger walked back to his car with the portfolio and the offer file in his hands. Stanley hadn't found anything in the language that could be misconstrued. The scary part was how easily Stanley had explained the process to Roger for how all twenty-three properties didn't have to stay in the loan as the debt was paid down.

"It's simple, Roger," said Stanley Russel, Esquire. "What you're worried about is called cross-collateraliza-tion. Plenty of times, a guy will bundle some properties and try to sell them, and then, if the buyer misses a payment in year ten or something, the seller will take all of them back. They won't give any quarter to the payments already made. They effectively screw the buyer out of everything they've paid, no matter how much equity they've built up. In other words, there's no provision for the buyer to clearly own individual assets as the equity increases."

Stanley indicated the seventh page of the offer file. "He's got it covered right here. You see where he indicates there is a title policy—actually an Owner's Title Policy—on each property? That's good. Now, here on the next page, he's assigned a specific value to each property based on the most recent appraisals, which were last year. I think those will still fly, but since this guy is bankrolling it, I don't think you should worry about it."

Roger looked up at his lawyer friend and nodded.

"Now, each property also has current surveys, including easements, and here, towards the end of the offer, see here? He's got specific amortization *and* depreciation schedules on each home. So, what you've got is here, in this clause—Section 16B in the contract—Release Provision. There's where you don't get screwed. Mr. Neiman has taken each property and assigned an extra 10% premium to it for it to be released and free from the debt of the overall mortgage."

Stanley looked up from Neiman's offer. "You said you have to put down what, 130 grand to close this deal?"

Roger nodded his head in agreement.

"Perfect. In theory, when you close on this contract, you could stipulate those monies go directly towards the ownership of certain specific homes in this deal and that would allow you to sell those outside of the private financing that governs the rest of the mortgage."

The puzzled look on Roger's face told Stanley he needed to explain it another way.

"Okay, Roger, let's say you go to the bank and ask them for a loan to buy twenty acres that you're going to subdivide and build homes on. Got me?"

"Yes."

"Now, let's say the bank didn't allow you to break off some of those pieces to sell—you'd have to pay off the entire loan before you could sell any of it. Follow me? That's called cross-collateralization. All the property is all the property.

"Actually, let me put it another way—every time you make a payment, the monies from that payment are directed towards equity in a specific piece of property. For you, as a layman, it might be easier to think of this contract, the way it is written, is simply a series of mortgages that you'll pay off one at a time."

Suddenly, Roger got it. "So, Louis' contract would allow me to sell off some of these homes if they were released? That way, I could improve others or just to keep my cash flow up in case of a downturn? As I pay down the principal of the entire loan, specific properties can be taken out of the contract and considered paid in full?"

"Yes! That's it in a nutshell. You'll pay a 10% premium on the value of the specific home in question, but yeah, that's the deal. A lot of seedy guys don't like doing that because they want to turn around and screw you after you've paid on stuff for years. Anyone that is upfront and honest would rather do this because the assets could, at least in theory, be paid for faster. It covers your ass, but it's not just from a sense of altruism. The lender doesn't want to get stuck with it, even if they could make all their money back again by selling the whole enchilada again in two years."

Stanley looked at Roger. "Now, I don't know who wrote this out, but they knew what they were doing. Any time you close on a deal like this, the costs are going to be more because you're buying twenty-three separate properties, but you've got a lot more information than a simple bundled deal. No matter how you close on this many properties, you're going to spend some coin at the attorneys. The way he's got this deal written, instead of two dozen or so separate closings, you'll have one long-assed one that treats the properties as separate."

Stanley looked at Roger. "So, are you going to do it? Roger, this thing is airtight. Even if it wasn't, the release clause means you can't get burned."

"I guess Susan and I have some talking to do tonight ..."

CHAPTER TWENTY-EIGHT

It is in your moments of decision
that your destiny is shaped.

—Tony Robbins

That same day, Susan had started off fuming. Roger needed to make a decision. He'd been analyzing for weeks and couldn't pull the trigger. Susan, on the other hand, had found the entire concept of real estate exciting, and it gave her a chance to create something real with her family and her husband.

He needed to tell Alliant to take a hike and that imbecile Fredericks could go down with his own ship. Not that he would. C-Level guys never got burned, but they sucked all the energy and money out of a company in the dire straits that Alliant was in and then landed somewhere else to put their experience to good use.

Around 9:30 a.m., she had a second cup of tea and calmed down. None of the negativity she was expending was going to amount to anything, and it would only cloud her judgment. She sat down and breathed deeply for a few minutes, repeated her own personal affirmations—she was happy that Roger was still doing his own also each morning and evening—and when she stopped, her blood pressure wasn't pounding in her head, and her mental state was clear.

Susan moved to the dining room table and went back over her copies of the portfolio and the offer Louis had provided.

* * * *

Roger walked in the door that evening at 6:35 p.m., and Susan met him there.

"Roger, we need to talk."

"Umm, okay, honey, can I get my other foot in the door?"

Susan would usually have smiled at a comment like that, but she didn't move. "Roger, I've made a decision, even if you won't. We're going to buy Neiman's properties. If I have to bootstrap the damned thing myself, I am going to do this. It's the only way we'll ever create real wealth or get you out of the damned sinking ship you work at, and jealously, I'm tired of being just a soccer mom. I know I can do this. I can run this damned thing like a champ inside of six months. Now, are you in or out?"

Roger was taken back by the emotion she expressed. Like any woman, she had her moments, but this? This was the woman who cried when she'd had to go back to work part time after the twins were born! Now she's angling to be the next real estate tycoon?

"Well, now that you've said all that, I wanted to tell you I met with Stanley Russel today."

"Roger, I don't care! You've been trying to shoot holes in this thing for six weeks! Either say yes or say no but *make a decision*. I already have."

"Susan, I did too. Yes. Call Louis and tell him yes."

CHAPTER TWENTY-NINE

A good decision is based on knowledge
and not on numbers.

—Plato

After all the fuss and stress, buying twenty-three houses from Louis Neiman proved to be nearly anticlimactic. They had spent an evening with John Gerber discussing how best to structure the company, and then Susan had simply gone online to create an LLC from the Secretary of State website. Next, they'd spent a couple hundred dollars to open checking accounts, transfer monies from the HELOC, the 401(k)s and the IRA, and two weeks later, Roger had taken off from work to spend the morning with Louis and his attorney while they signed what seemed like an endless stream of documents.

Louis had agreed to stay in town for at least the first month, mentoring Susan on the day-to-day operations.

Then, he would simply make himself available to the Alcotts via Skype as they needed him.

When Roger and Susan got up from the closing table, they owned two rental properties free and clear and had slightly more than $1.1 million in debt on eighteen more. None of those houses were new, none of them were beautiful, but all of them were leased and had long term tenants in them and were producing, on average, over $650 each month in positive cashflow.

John Gerber had taken the time to introduce them to his property manager, Tom Cullen, whom Roger finally realized was the man he'd seen driving the grey Chevy in the weeks before the Gerbers had moved into their home.

"Tom is what an old Navy friend of mine calls a dog robber—he gets things done. If you need to get a plumber on a Christmas Eve, Tom can find him. If you need an oddball capacitor for a long, obsolete air conditioner, Tom finds one. Men like him make our jobs a lot easier."

Gerber had said if Roger or Susan had any questions or needed a second opinion about something that Louis' contractors said, they could feel free to call on Tom for his advice.

Painfully aware of their own lack of knowledge about property management, they knew how valuable this was.

Overall, though, the first weeks of owning rentals proved to be busy but not exciting. Susan spent her days in the dining room office transferring information from Louis' systems to Alcott Limited, LLC—the name they had chosen for their LLC, and at least to Susan, Brent, and Chris, the most boring name in the world. Susan had upgraded QuickBooks and bought a management software—a CRM—to use to send out rent notices, pay bills, and allow their contractors to submit their invoices.

Personally, she'd had fun envisioning how all these things would work together. She'd even started creating an operations' manual in a binder—on the spine of it, she'd handwritten "How We Do It Here" and was slowly filling it up with processes she'd begun adapting from Louis Neiman.

The first call from a tenant had actually been for a broken water heater nearly two weeks after Susan and Roger had taken over the company. Susan had called their plumbing contractor, explained what was going on, and he had told her when he'd be on site and what to ask the tenant to do in the meantime.

She'd thanked him, hung up the phone, called back the tenant, and then, after hanging up with him, had opened the file on the house, noted the water heater was still under a factory warranty, and texted that information back to the contractor.

Two and a half hours later, he'd called back to tell her the problem was solved.

Susan had giggled. This was easy! She knew they'd have challenges of course, but since Louis had a system, and the Alcotts were essentially following that system, she (and she was sure, Roger) felt confident they'd be able to find the right answer if a real problem arose.

In his Alliant office, Roger didn't quite share his wife's optimism. Sure, they were making some money, and they had a system, but he knew that if he didn't start to generate new income with the real estate business, it would take years to escape Alliant.

He spun his chair around to look out at the Atlanta skyline, draped in the grey skies of a February day.

They *had* to start wholesaling. If he could get that part of Alcott Limited off the ground, he could tell Jenkins to kiss off. Louis had said you got one in every twenty deals, so that meant he'd have to generate forty leads—forty motivated sellers—each month.

He made a note to ask Louis or John where they had their signs printed and who they had used successfully for direct mail marketing, and he knew he had to move on that quickly. He needed buyers, too, but he and Susan had identified nearly twenty companies in Atlanta that had assured Roger they were motivated buyers used to wholesaled transactions and assigned contracts. Even Gerber had checked off on most of them, reinforcing the idea that Roger and Susan had a buyers list—maybe not the biggest one but a list, nonetheless.

As he drove home later that evening, Roger remembered his ride through his own neighborhood with John. The man had pointed out houses that could be wholesaled and Roger, caught up in the last six weeks with his own real estate business, had no idea if Gerber's company had bought them, approached them, or done any business.

Tapping his Bluetooth, he called Gerber to at least leave a message. Surprisingly, the man answered.

"Hello, Roger! How is the newest real estate tycoon?"

"I'm great, John, thanks. Hey, I was thinking back to our drive a few weeks ago when you'd pointed out houses here in the subdivision. Did you guys ever move forward with those? I need to get started in this wholesaling business, and I'd like to see if you and I can chat sometime."

Gerber chuckled into the phone. "Actually, Roger, even with the holidays and travel and all that is going on in my world, I still did. Nobody wanted to play ball."

He dodged a possum waddling in the road by the clubhouse and asked Gerber if he'd have some time in the next few evenings to talk about marketing and wholesaling. Gerber invited him to stop in the next night—Patricia had something going on with her gal pals, and he would be left all alone for a couple hours. Roger agreed to meet John at 6:30 the next night.

Before he hung up, John did tell Roger the name of the company that he bought all his signs from and the names of the companies that handled his direct mail marketing and the answering service that fielded sales calls.

Twenty-three hours later, John opened the back door for Roger, and the two men shook hands. John handed him three pieces of paper.

"This is what you're looking for, Roger. It's a copy of the standard contract I've used for years. You and Susan can steal all the verbiage on it. This one was written specifically for homes owned free and clear. I can't tell you to get involved with houses that have debt; it can get convoluted. Suffice it to say, that's another whole ball of wax."

"Damn, that was easy," said Roger, smiling. "Thank you. I know Louis had one in his files that he's shared, but I've been so worried about handling and anticipating challenges from the rental side. I haven't made the time to ask him about it."

"Roger, it's really quite simple. You understand the ARV—the after repaired value—and essentially, you fill in the blanks."

Roger read the document, amazed that something so concise was all that was needed to buy and sell a home if banks weren't involved.

Gerber pointed at a single line at the bottom of the page. "Here's where the magic happens, Roger, 'Number Nine—Other Provisions.'"

The man read the language, "Seller acknowledges that Buyer is purchasing the Property in an attempt to make a profit. This agreement is binding to the Seller, Buyer, and their heirs, legal representatives, successors, and assigns ..."

"Get it, Roger? That's the Assignment Clause, which is so critical to our business. Different states require different language, but they all come to the same point. The buyer can assign—or sell—the contract. At the same time, if you look, you'll see that the so-called Inspection Clause allows you, as a buyer, to get out of the contract if you absolutely have to; for example, if you cannot find a buyer. Now, are you going to quit goofing around and put out some signs? You can't buy what you can't find."

"John, we're going to. It's just ... how? I mean, I get it—put the signs out and wait for people to call. Just ..." He let the sentence trail off.

"Just," John responded, "you aren't sure how to approach someone to tell them their house is worth a fraction of the price of the one across the street?"

Roger nodded. "Yes, that's a part of it. But when do I do that? I'm sitting in an office all day. Susan? Sure, she can do it, but I don't want her to go somewhere unsafe. Who knows what can happen?"

"Well, Roger, that's a part of it, of course, but think about it—how many things can be done by phone? People call and don't have all their information; they don't understand the game or the numbers. Susan can field those calls until you get your answering service set up, using a checklist of things to ask and vet any caller long before you—or even her—would set foot on a property. If she has a potential deal, she calls you, gets you the information, and you go visit the house on your way home from work."

"In the dark?" asked Roger.

"If that's what it takes. When someone calls us, understand they are ready to sell. They are up against something—time, money, family, even legal issues. Your number isn't the first or the last number they'll dial. You have to get there and start the process. Even if you have to come back the next day. Sure, it's easier when the days are longer, and it's not dark at 5:30 p.m. like it is today but do something now. Get motivated and take responsibility, or you'll have another excuse in a month. Remember Jack Canfield and his E+R=O formula?"

Gerber's words cut Roger, but he knew they were true. As hard charging as he was in sales at Alliant, he was also coming from a place of experience and confidence. He knew the logistics business; he didn't know real estate. He *really* didn't know flipping real estate.

The voice in his head laughed and added a *that's the damn truth, Rog*.

John looked at Roger and smiled. "Here, I'll throw down the gauntlet. Come with me."

Roger followed Gerber out to his garage where he walked over to a stack of blank yellow signs. He took out eight of them.

"Get one of the extra fat Sharpie markers, neatly write out how you guys buy ugly houses, and place these out this weekend. On a couple of them, change the message to reflect a three-bedroom house you have for sale for—let's say, $59,000. Do this tonight and put these out Friday night. Call me when the phone rings."

Roger tried to put up an argument, but as he opened his mouth to say something, the garage door began opening. Patricia was home.

He smiled and said, "What timing! Now go, Roger, and make some real money. You've only scratched the surface!"

Roger said a brief hello and goodbye to Patricia, thanked John again, and walked back to his house.

It was time to get moving.

CHAPTER THIRTY

Many a small thing has been made large
by the right kind of advertising.

—Mark Twain

Roger, Susan, and the twins all aided in the design of their first round of bandit signs. Not completely sure what to write, Susan had looked up the various ones she had photographed in her travels, and they arrived at what they thought was a series of good messages.

At the very least, Susan joked, they'd know what didn't work by the end of the weekend.

Friday morning, after checking emails and verifying two pieces of work contractors had taken care of the previous day, Susan dialed the number for the answering service that John Gerber had recommended. She was more than a little taken back to find that they would not only direct and vet any callers—they could also set up several different phone numbers that

Susan and Roger could use for business to keep their personal numbers private. They had a one-time setup fee, then a flat monthly fee based on usage. The young lady, Ginger, directed Susan to the company website, then walked her through the process.

In the end, as expensive as an answering service sounded, it cost next to nothing, and the team would use John Gerber's questionnaire (subtly edited by Susan for the Alcotts) to vet all callers, then they could simply email the questionnaire to Susan.

Susan was amazed at how easy technology had made this! She completed the form, hit send, and in two minutes, Ginger confirmed that the payment had gone through, and Susan and Roger had an answering service set up for Alcott Limited. Ginger explained it would be twenty-four to forty-eight hours before everything was fully transferred, but she felt confident that Sunday morning, by approximately 10:30 a.m., the phones would be ringing at the call center. She would be their account manager, and if they had any challenges, Susan or Mr. Alcott could reach out on Ginger's direct line or via email.

Unbelievable!

Friday night, the family loaded up the car with the signs they had made the previous evening, went out to dinner, and then set out the signs. With a flourish, Chris and Brent had placed each sign. Susan logged the location of each sign on her phone. After all the signs were placed, Roger took the whole clan out for ice cream.

Halfway through dessert, the phone rang with their first potential sale.

* * * *

Saturday afternoon, Ginger had called to verify the answering service was prepared to shift the lines, and sure enough, the ping of emails replaced the ring of Susan's phone.

By the end of the weekend, the Alcotts and their team had fielded no less than forty-four calls on their signs, and of those, Roger and Susan were left with a list of nine sellers and three buyers. Susan had made appointments Sunday afternoon with five of the sellers they'd spoken to on Friday night and Saturday. The first two proved to be challenging. The homes were unoccupied and falling apart. The roof had begun to collapse on one, and the windows were broken out of the other—along with the air conditioner having been stolen. Nonetheless, Roger had run comps in the area, dutifully plugged in numbers on Louis' cheat sheet, and after an hour or so, had been able to calculate an offer for the seller.

The offers were immediately rejected both times. *Damn.*

Couldn't these folks see that what they were selling was in terrible shape? Couldn't they understand the sheer amount of work necessary to make these homes livable? His offers had still been well above the land value of the property but accurate reflections of the time and work necessary to repair the houses.

As he sat in the car, fuming, a red car drove by.

He remembered Louis Neiman's red car example.

Roger smiled, started the car, and called the next owner to tell him they were on their way.

Houses number three, four, and five were as disappointing as the first two. Nevertheless, Roger had gone through what he now thought of as his system and produced an offer. He wasn't surprised the offers were rejected, but he began to feel less nervous about it. Susan had proven to be perfectly suited for this, sharing her ideas as a woman on how the house could be remodeled, what she would want done to it to make her comfortable as a mother, and generally softening the edges of what was, in the end, a very dry exchange of information.

Roger realized that he wasn't building rapport with people; he was simply crunching numbers. His side of the transaction might be all about numbers, but it dawned on him, sitting with Susan at the stoplight after leaving the fifth house, that for the sellers, this was an emotional time.

They were selling the home they had raised their children in or the one they had been raised in. They had memories in these homes, just like he did in his own. He had to be hard on his numbers, but he had to be more respectful of the situation these sellers were in.

As they drove, the ping of a lead buzzed on Susan's phone. Susan opened it, read through it, and then returned the call. She pulled out a notepad and began taking notes about what Roger knew had to be another house. She thanked the person on the other end of the line and closed out the call with "we'll see you in about half an hour" and hung up.

"Pull over, Roger—we got one!"

Roger pulled into the parking lot of a gas station, and Susan immediately pulled out her iPad and started punching up the address.

The house was actually located on the same road as their subdivision but was an older home developed when the area had first started to really grow in the early eighties. Fifteen minutes later, Susan had three comps, the tax assessor's report on the property, and knew that the lady who had just called them was the original owner of the home whose husband had passed away eighteen months before.

"Let's go. This is the one!" Susan said, laughing as they pulled into traffic.

Six minutes later, a lady named Valerie Browning answered the door to her home. She looked, for all the world, like an archetypical grandmother, all the way down to her glasses and apron.

She let them into a neat living room, offered them coffee or tea, and then started talking.

She and her husband Shawn had bought the house new in 1984 and had lived there ever since. Their son had grown up there, gone to college at Georgia State, and now lived in Knoxville, "doing something in technology."

Shawn had gone to bed one night a year and a half ago, complaining of indigestion and simply never woken up. Now a widow, Valerie had thought about selling the house, but the two different real estate agents she'd talked to last year had been "slick talking little bastards" who turned her off listing with them or their companies. She'd tried to figure out how to sell the house herself but wasn't even sure where to begin.

As she spoke, it sank in to Roger that in order to buy this house, he and Susan would really have to gain Valerie's trust. He couldn't just run numbers and make an offer—to her, this was *home*. He'd need to share with her how he and Susan arrived at a number and then confidently express that number to her. The three of them had been talking for nearly half an hour when Roger decided to try his hand at creating an offer.

"Mrs. Browning, the way we work is simple. First of all, you deal with Susan and me directly in all this. We don't hide behind lawyers and fancy talk; we have a simple contract that is written in plain English. Our process is simple. We look at homes in the area—new and old—to understand how homes are valued. Now, may I speak freely?"

Valerie Browning nodded her head.

"Ma'am, you've got an older home that seems to be in nice shape. With your permission, I'd like to take a more in-depth look at it. Things like the air conditioner, the roof, the exterior, and then, if you'd allow it, look through the rest of the house as well. You are more than welcome to walk with me, and as we go through this, I'm sure, if nothing else, you'll be able to understand any challenges the house has. I'm sure you can guess how important that is, not only from our point of view but also from yours. By the time we're done, I can not only give you an offer on the house, but you would also know what another buyer might see that holds them back from purchasing it. Does that make sense?"

"Roger, take all the time you need and go wherever you need. There's a crawl space access door on the backside. Susan, would you like another cup of tea?"

It took Roger nearly an hour to fill in his pricing sheet. In the end, he'd found the air conditioner was actually an ancient heat pump far past its useful life, the roof was ten years old but in good shape, and there was no evidence of water in the attic or the crawl space. The appliances all had manufacture dates from 2002–2003, and judging from the decor in the house, he guessed that Valerie and Shawn had spent money that year updating the interior.

Roger walked in the front door from making his calculations in the car to the sound of the women laughing, and he cautiously moved into the living room.

"I'm back! Mrs. Browning, thank you again for reaching out to us. I can't imagine losing my wife, and I hate the thought of my sons growing up. I've made a lot of mistakes in how I used my time when they were little boys, but now I love coming home to my family. May I go over my report with you?"

She looked at Roger, then looked at Susan and smiled. "Yep, lay it on me." Then, she started laughing.

Just like he had several other times that day, Roger began trying to explain how he'd arrived at the price. Valerie cut him off, "Roger, for Heaven's sake, skip down to the good part. I've lived here for over thirty years; I know all about this place."

Caught off guard, Roger looked up. "Yes ma'am. Well, the bottom line is that we'd be prepared to offer you $110,765 cash for your home. If you feel the price is fair, we can get the whole process started with your signature right here, and assuming our due diligence is all correct and verified, we can close inside of two weeks."

Valerie looked puzzled. "What an odd number. Wow! Two weeks? How long would I have to actually move?"

Roger was caught off guard again. "As a general rule, within seventy-two hours of closing, but if you needed extra time, we could give you up to two more weeks."

"No, it's a deal. This has been a fantastic home, but it's time to move on. I've been here forever, and now, it's time to turn the page." And with that, Valerie Browning reached over, picked up the Zebra pen, and signed the contract.

CHAPTER THIRTY-ONE

*Success is going from failure to failure
without losing enthusiasm.*

—Winston Churchill

The rest of Sunday passed in a hazy blur. The Alcotts picked up their bandit signs, and Roger and Susan, ecstatic but terrified, suddenly realized the challenge they faced.

They had a signed contract and no buyer, and they didn't have the liquidity to buy the house themselves. Roger didn't sleep well that night, but he noticed that Susan fell asleep almost instantly.

Monday at Alliant was a prison to Roger. He had plenty of things to do for *that* job, but the contract with Valerie Browning was making him nearly sick to his stomach. He knew that Susan was calling their woefully short list of buyers they had created, but having not heard anything from her, his mind imagined a

191

steady string of noes in response to her calls. Finally, thankfully, he left Alliant, drove home, and immediately walked over to the Gerbers' house.

Of course, the man wasn't home.

Patricia had answered and was excited that Roger and Susan had gotten their first contract but couldn't—or wouldn't—offer any advice. Louis Neiman also was conspicuously absent when Roger had called.

Despite their new rules about no business talk at the table, Roger and Susan monopolized the conversation with talk of the Browning house. Susan had tried everyone on their buyer's list but only heard back from three of them.

All had said, "No, thanks."

There were still over a dozen more, but Roger's experience with people not calling you back in business meant they weren't interested either.

Tuesday didn't start out much better. John had called Roger to congratulate him on his first contract, but the call dropped, and Roger's return calls went immediately to voicemail.

Damn.

Tuesday at Alliant, Roger again felt like a prisoner. He had to get this contract sold! He couldn't worry about a truckload of televisions being offloaded in San Diego. Gerber was obviously dodging him, and the little voices in his own head were having a field day.

Way to go, Rog, now you're gonna screw the widow out of the solution you sold her.

Rog, you're a logistics guy, not a real estate guy. Stay in your lane!

Alliant needs you to fix it, not chase bumblebees; what do you know about real estate?

Roger noted grimly that the last voice sounded a lot like Clayton Fredericks.

By the time he left work, Roger's blood pressure was pounding in his ears, and abandoning any semblance of civility, he simply pulled into Gerber's driveway and knocked on the front door.

No, he *pounded* on the front door.

Gerber answered. "Roger? How are you? What's wrong?"

"John, I can't sell this damn house! You convinced me that I could change everything; you gave me *Four Entrepreneurial Freedoms* and Money, Deals, and People, and then Louis' houses have what feels like every penny I own attached to them. I reached out to you today, and when the call dropped, you disappeared. What the hell am I going to do?"

John Gerber had seen more than one new investor freaked out by the financial stress of starting their real estate business, so he was no stranger to these questions.

"Well, Roger, the answer is quite simple. You have to sell the house. And I didn't call you back, because honestly, I'd dropped the damned phone in the toilet."

Gerber's honesty—and the absurdity of his answer—suddenly broke the tension Roger had been feeling since he and Susan had left Valerie Browning's house.

"Just like that? I'll find someone to assign this contract to who will buy this thing for $130 grand or so? We've been trying. Nobody wants it. Everyone has said no. Even worse, no one has even given me a second look, to meet me at the house, to do a walk through. I know it's worth it, but nobody wants to give it a look."

John Gerber looked at Roger Alcott. "Well, for starters, Roger, you aren't saddled with the house—you've got the Inspection Clause that offers you a way out if you cannot find a buyer to assign the contract to. So, you're covered—"

Roger cut him off, "John, you don't get it—I *have* to sell this house. I understand—I guess—how I'm not financially obligated to buy it based on the Inspection Clause, but ... I don't know. I just feel that if I don't step up and do this ... Hell, John, you taught me this. I have a responsibility to sell this house, not only to my seller but to my family."

"Roger, I appreciate what you're saying, but if you're going to have a coronary over it, then selling it will do you no good. Remember, they're called the *Four Entrepreneurial Freedoms*, not the *Four Entrepreneurial* Shackles. Now, who have you contacted?"

Roger listed off the names and then sighed. The list wasn't very long.

Gerber leaned in. "Roger, I know every one of those guys, and every one of them is a flipper. They'll buy the house, but they buy one at a time. Small timers. You need some people who are renting properties—the same model Louis used."

John ticked off the names of three or four men who might have an interest in a property like the one Roger had and said, "I know this whole process—learning the real estate business as an investor—is like drinking from a firehose, but if I remember correctly, you haven't ever visited any of our local investor meet-ups, have you?"

Gerber had explained it was an important part of the networking that the business relied upon, but Roger, caught up in Alliant drama and the deal with

Louis, had never taken the time to attend one. There was a standing meeting every Thursday afternoon at a local restaurant. The way John had described it, it was like the Kiwanis Club meeting the chamber of commerce.

"John, I'm in the office then. I can't just up and leave to go to a meeting about real estate."

"Are you going to work for Alliant forever? Would they begrudge you a few hours as an executive to go handle some personal business? Are you paid hourly?"

Gerber knew the answers to all of these questions, and Roger did too.

"Roger, I know that deep down you're always going to be a company man. You like systems and processes, clear documentation, and in your former life—the life at Alliant—that path was clear. Now, though, you're making up your own systems. Sure, you've got the one that Louis worked out and the suggestions I've made, but ultimately, the business you and Susan are building is *yours*. You own it, and you own the results. At Alliant …?" He let the question hang, and Roger picked it up.

"… I just own the results."

"So, we'll see you Thursday at the REI meeting?"

"Yes, sir. I guess you will."

And with that, the two men shook hands, and Roger moved his car and parked in his own driveway.

CHAPTER THIRTY-TWO

*Speak in such a way that others love
to listen to you. Listen in such a way
that others love to speak to you.*

—Zig Ziglar

If there was one thing Roger Alcott could do, it was work a room. At least, that's what he'd thought. He'd gotten to the Real Estate Investor's Association meeting Thursday afternoon with the intention of making as many contacts as he could. He figured it would be an easy deal, and Tuesday night, after his meltdown with John Gerber, he'd talked himself up pretty well.

As the REI meeting came to a close, though, Roger could feel the frustration seeping into his mind. All the positive affirmations in the world couldn't seem to get him back into a better disposition, but he couldn't lie. He *had* met about thirty-two people who were all buying, flipping, and renting multiple properties.

John had introduced him to many of them, but Roger had managed to meet a few people while Gerber was talking to others.

A few of the ones he'd met knew him due to his purchase of Louis's portfolio and seemed supportive. Quite a few were off in sidebar conversations that the sales professional in Roger knew meant money was going to change hands. Despite meeting people, exchanging business cards, and rubbing elbows with these folks, Roger left the meeting with his contract untouched, and no one begging for him to sell them Valerie Browning's house.

The next day, he dutifully pushed papers around on his desk at Alliant, answered a few emails, and followed up on sales calls and emails the rest of the day. However, the Browning contract was weighing heavily on his mind. Driving home, he called John Gerber on his Bluetooth.

Gerber answered, "Roger, how are you? I hope you were able to get some value out of the REI meeting— sometimes it's like being the new kid in class. Most of us know each other, and in some cases, we've known each other for years."

"I'm frustrated, John. I thought … I don't know *what* I thought, but I guess I'd hoped to meet someone there who could buy the house. I know it's worth more than I paid for it; I just don't know who to sell it to."

"Actually, Roger, it is a solid first contract. You struck a great deal, and I promise someone is going to fall all over themselves for that house before you have to fall on your sword and lean on the inspection clause."

Suddenly, Roger had what he thought was a brilliant idea. "John, what would *you* buy the house for?

I'm on my way home now, and I can walk the contract over this evening."

"No, no, no, Roger. Listen to yourself. You sound desperate. You're going to be fine. And please, don't take offense, but I would never do business with someone I've tried to teach. Inevitably, they think I'm screwing them out of money, or people in our business think that. It's bad for one's reputation, especially given how small of a community we really are. To me, the mentor-protégé relationship is sacred. It's far too important to screw it up with houses."

"John, how do I sell this damned thing? I mean, I've still got plenty of time, but the uncertainty of it? It's killing me."

"Roger, it will if you let it, I assure you. The first one is always the hardest. Have you or Susan heard back from any of the other investors on the list?"

"Yes, four more noes and a few 'I can't right now's.' That's pretty much the end of the list. Susan has been working the phone all week, and I know she's nervous. It's like I said the other night—it won't impact us financially, but we both understand that if we're going to make real money in real estate, we've got to be able to move from signed contract to closed business."

"Roger, you're a smart guy. Why are you beating yourself up? It's not like you have to buy the damned thing if the closing date gets here, and you haven't found a buyer."

"Yes, I understand that. You and Louis drove that into my head and explained how the language reads in these contracts. It's just … I've got to do this. If I can't make this system work, then everything is for nothing. I mean, yes, we'll have income, but if I can't wholesale houses or add to my own portfolio of investments, then all I've done is send Susan back to work."

"What was the address again, Roger?"

Roger rattled the number and street off and then, as he always seemed to, John Gerber said goodbye, leaving Roger Alcott to drive home with a house on his shoulders.

* * *

Dinner at the Alcott home had always been fairly reserved. Susan never allowed the boys to become rowdy, and until recently, Roger usually missed dinner, so the Alcott family had evolved into a fairly quiet routine. Each member of the family was expected to discuss their day and share five wins they had, no matter how small those were.

Susan had made meatloaf, and despite the fact Roger loved it, that night, she couldn't help but notice the man had taken a far smaller slice then usual and was intently pushing around most of the food on his plate. When his turn came to share about his day, Roger had halfheartedly fallen back on positives like his sons, his family, and their time together.

Sitting at the family table, Roger looked physically smaller. Susan was worried. If the pressure of selling one contract caused this, what would it be like if he was trying to do this all the time? She knew they had a lot to learn in the business, but she had long ago taken up with the philosophy to make the best of anything you got; in the end, hard work and diligence would get you through anything.

As the boys were clearing off the table, the doorbell rang.

Chris dashed off to answer it, and Roger heard the deep voice of John Gerber saying hello to their son and asking if his mom and dad were home.

He ran back into the kitchen to report what Roger and Susan already knew and just as quickly ran back to the door to tell John that yes, yes indeed, his parents were home.

Susan walked into the foyer to meet John and was surprised to find her neighbor wasn't alone. With him stood a thin wisp of a man impeccably dressed in what was obviously a custom-made suit. John stepped into the foyer and introduced the other gentleman as Clive Jones.

Jones reached out his hand to take Susan's and shook it at the same moment Roger walked through the door. Turning gracefully, Jones extended his hand to Roger's, and Roger, no stranger to the hearty grasp of a firm handshake, was impressed with it and Jones' eye contact.

There was the faintest hint of an accent, but Roger couldn't place it.

Jones cut right to the chase. "Mr. and Mrs. Alcott, I'm terribly sorry to interrupt your evening. If I may be blunt, John has informed me that you've got a house locally under contract. I'd be very interested in it if the price were right. May I inject myself into your evening for a few moments?"

Roger nearly fell over. Susan's smile grew obscenely large. In unison, they stammered out, "Why, yes, you can!"

John smiled and looked at Clive Jones. "Clive, I think I'll step back over to the house and leave you here. If you need me, I'll be up until about 10:30 p.m., but I'm sure you'll be gone well before then."

Jones looked offended. "10:30 p.m.? My dear Gerber, I wouldn't dare to bother these good folks so late. I'm sure we'll only be a few moments, and I'll be off myself."

Gerber closed the door as he left, and Susan sprang into full hostess mode.

"Mr. Jones, may I get you a cup of tea? Coffee? Perhaps something stronger? None of it would be any trouble."

"Aye, thank you, ma'am, but I've still got a bit of work to do at home too. Plus, the missus would think I've been laid up in a pub if I came home with one on my breath. No, I'll not need a drink, but if you'd join me with a cup of tea, I'll take an Earl Grey if you have it?"

"That's my favorite, too, Mr. Jones. Give me a moment, and I'll get a pot going."

Roger had regained his wits and escorted Clive Jones into the living room, shooing the twins out of it. He offered a seat on the couch to the visitor, who took it, again apologizing for the lateness of his visit.

"Mr. Alcott, I'll try to value your time and get quickly to the point. John has shared with me that you have a contract on a home close by, specifically on Brittany Drive. Is that correct?"

"Yes, sir, Mr. Jo—Clive. The owner and I signed it not quite a week ago, and I'd like to find a buyer to assign it to. Did John tell you anything about my wife and me?"

"Well, he let on that you had bought Louis' properties and were new in the wholesaling game, but he said that your previous experience in sales made you a bit shrewd at the closing table." Jones let out a chuckle and added, "He did allow that this contract was causing you some degree of concern, but he chalked it up to the drama of your current position at Alliant. I certainly hope John's lack of formality doesn't offend you; he really thinks quite highly of you and your wife."

Roger was taken aback at the sideways compliment John had paid him through Clive Jones. *Maybe this old dog can learn a new trick,* said the voice in his head.

Jones wasted little time. "Roger, I'll put it simply. I know this area very well. I've bought or sold, I don't know, thirty-four—thirty-five—homes within just a few miles of here in the last few years—ever since the market fell apart. Assuming that your ARV is on the spot—and I'd like to subject-to that before I leave here in a few moments—I'd like to ask you to let me inspect the property at your leisure tomorrow, once you've cleared it with the homeowner. If those numbers make sense, then I'd like to purchase the contract."

Roger was caught completely off guard. Who the hell shows up after dinner and asks to buy a home they'd only just found out about? He smiled, then found his voice. "Why yes, yes, I think I can arrange that for you, Clive. What time would be best?"

"Well, I can avail myself to you anytime. Why not call your seller first thing and then call me? I can meet your guys out there at their convenience."

"That's great, Clive, I've got—" *to work tomorrow,* said Roger's inner voice, and just as quickly, a new voice, deeper and more mature, took over in Roger's head … *to hell with that! I've got a deal to close with this Limey*—"some free time in the late morning or the afternoon, so once I call my seller, I'll ring you back? Will that work?"

Jones nodded, reached into his jacket pocket, and pulled out an alligator business card holder. As he did, Roger caught the label on the inside of the jacket. Burberry on New Bond Street in London. Clive Jones certainly seemed like a guy who would fly to England for his clothes. Unlike many of the cards Roger had handled, this one was notably thicker and heavily embossed. On it was only "Clive Jones—Real Estate Investor" and the man's phone number. No email, no address.

Susan brought in the tea, sat with the men for a few minutes, and then excused herself to get the boys squared away for the evening.

Jones asked a few more questions about the property—the condition of the overall structure, how the owner was or wasn't taking care of it, and Roger's opinion of the house. Would he let his family or a friend move into it as it sat, or would he have to renovate it before doing so?

Roger tried to answer Jones' questions truthfully and preface his answers, but he understood what Jones was doing—he was gauging the degree of work needed on the Browning house based on what a man like Roger would do if it was on the market.

Finally, after what seemed like an hour but by the clock on the wall had only been twenty-three minutes, Jones looked at his own watch, stood up, and apologized for monopolizing the Alcotts' evening. He shook Roger's hand, asked him to tell his wife goodnight, and reminded Roger again to call as soon as he had spoken to the homeowner in the morning.

Just as quickly as he had arrived, Clive Jones was gone back into the late February evening that had brought him to the Alcott home.

* * * *

Neither Roger nor Susan slept well that night, and they had stayed up late pondering the mysterious Clive Jones. Where had John dug him up? Who was he? What would he be prepared to offer on the house? They talked until nearly two in the morning and then fell into their own dreamless sleeps.

When he awoke, Roger realized today was the day. When the sun set, he and Susan would either be one step closer to realizing their dream, or the stress would likely have killed him. Along the way, though, he still had a few challenges. What if Valerie Browning wasn't home? What if Jones didn't like the house? What if his offer was below what Roger had valued the house?

When the hell *was* he going to be able to meet Jones at the house since he had to be at Alliant that day?

The last question was the one that really bothered him. Not that his team couldn't handle the tasks they were appointed to do. He would be minutes away from the office, in reality, but the fact that he wasn't in the office somehow made him nervous ... like the shareholders were going to suddenly appear and demand justice for Roger deserting his post.

Thinking back to his last few conversations with Clayton Fredericks, Roger's jaw suddenly set, and his face seemed to harden. "To hell with Fredericks and the whole lot of them," he said out loud. He had figured out months ago that Alliant was dying a slow death, and the only ones who were going to win anything in the fight were the attorneys. The bonus he'd been working toward? Gone in a memo on January 3. The raise Fredericks had promised? Pushed into the second quarter, at least.

No, Alliant was a lost cause, and even though Roger Alcott knew that, he still felt a pang of guilt at the thought of leaving his office in the middle of the day.

But I'll do it if I have to, said the new inner voice. You can call me New Roger, and things are going to change around here.

* * * *

In the end, the newer, more assertive version of Roger Alcott didn't need to do anything. Susan called Valerie Browning and explained they had a gentleman who was interested in the house whom they'd like to show it to, and if possible, could she leave them alone for an hour or so? Susan would be happy to buy her lunch if she didn't have any plans, but Valerie said she had some shopping to do and would be out from about 10:30 a.m. until 1:00 p.m. Would that work?

Susan thought, *You bet!* But she only thanked the lady and asked where she would leave a key for them.

As soon as she hung up the phone, she texted Roger, and when he got the text, he called Clive Jones.

Roger pulled up at the Browning house at quarter of eleven, and four minutes later, an older Mercedes 850 pulled up to the curb. This morning had dawned cold and clear, and despite the fact March was only days away, winter still felt very close. Jones got out of his car dressed in, of all things, a tweed coat and khaki trousers with leather boots, which likely cost more than Roger's first car.

The men shook hands, and Clive cut right to the chase. "I knew it! This is why I buy these houses. The builder! This is his work. Fantastic man, Jim Arnold. He built dozens of homes around here from about 1979 to about 1985. These homes are like tanks. He overbuilt these things from the start. Let's take a walk, shall we, Roger?"

For the next forty-five minutes, Clive Jones gave Roger a lesson in construction. He pointed out where Arnold had used thicker lumber in floor and ceiling joists, heavier exterior doors, and in a time long before home computers and multiple phones in a home were common, Arnold had thoughtfully included enough electrical outlets and ground faults to ensure safety throughout the electrical systems of his homes.

Roger felt optimistic as he and Clive Jones walked out to the curb. Jones excused himself to review his notes, and Roger knew this was the moment of truth.

While Jones sat in the Mercedes, Roger checked his phone. There was a message from his secretary about a minor setback on a delivery to Lincoln due to blizzard conditions on I-80 but nothing unusual. He looked up from his phone as he heard the car door close.

"Roger, you said this closes next Monday, correct?"

Alcott nodded. "Yes, sir. We wrote paper on it on a Sunday, so Monday was the best I could hope for. You said you knew the attorney, didn't you?"

"Absolutely. We've done considerable business together over the years. All right, Roger. Now that I've see the house, I can't do better than $127,000."

Roger Alcott looked at Clive Jones. In all the chatter, he suddenly realized he had never put a price on it!

"I ... I," he stammered and then caught himself. "Sold! Mr. Jones, I appreciate it."

The two men shook hands. Jones waited a few minutes and then said, "Umm, Roger, chap, you *do* have a contract for me, don't you?"

Damn! In his haste to get all his ducks in a row, he had left it sitting on the end of the counter that morning. "Clive, honestly, with all the stuff going on, I do, but I left it at my house this morning. Could I meet you later and give it to you? I could have Susan run it by your office. I can't believe it! I'm really sorry."

"Roger, no worries! Yes, by all means, have Susan fill it out, and I can even pick it up this evening. I have two appointments this afternoon. Perhaps we could meet after those? You tell me—you're the man helping me out. May I ask you a favor, though?"

"Of course, Clive."

"Would you be opposed to picking up the check for the assignment fee at the closing attorney's the day we close?"

Roger was taken aback. He hadn't thought about *that*. "Sure, that's no problem. I mean, if it's okay, I was planning on coming by to talk to Joel about the closing process that day, anyhow; I ... I've got some questions about this whole thing too."

"Perfect, thank you, Roger."

They agreed to meet at a small restaurant not far from the Alcott home at six that evening, and Roger, ecstatic over having assigned the contract, spent the next six hours worrying about getting a signature.

He didn't need to. Despite all the worry, at six o'clock, they found Clive Jones sitting at a corner booth nursing a soft drink and waiting for them. He signed the contract, and the three sat chatting amiably for another half hour, then got up, said their goodbyes, and walked to their cars.

Roger fairly fell into the seat of the Lexus. Susan giggled like a girl. They looked at one another and laughed aloud. "That was $17,000 over a drink!" said Roger.

Susan smiled. "Well, over ten days. Make that closer to fifteen. But still damn good work if you can find it."

Roger Alcott slept like a baby that night.

CHAPTER THIRTY-THREE

Plans are nothing; planning is everything.

—Dwight D. Eisenhower

At his core, Roger was a planner. He liked the surety of knowing how things worked. He relished understanding systems and processes and then using those to make money. For years, as a salesman, he had relied on not only knowing *when* shipments were unloaded, manifests booked, and orders placed but also *how* the entire thing worked. Over his twenty-year career, he'd used that information and knowledge to make sure his customers stayed happy with all aspects of the services his company provided.

As he and Susan had begun learning the real estate investment business, he found himself far from his safe places and knew the only way he could ever feel truly confident in his new venture was to learn the entire process and understand the system.

When he knew that, he could provide value to his tenants, his buyers, and his sellers.

If he could do that, he could capitalize on every part of the transaction and ensure people enjoyed the experience he and Susan were giving them when they dealt with Alcott Limited.

All this ran through his mind in a near constant loop over the weekend, and late Sunday afternoon, he decided he needed to play an active role in the closing process to learn exactly how it worked, rather than simply assign a contract, show up at the attorney's office, and collect a check.

John Gerber, Louis Neiman, and even the attorney handling this close, Joel Habersham, had answered question after question about how the process worked, but Roger still didn't feel 100% confident in his understanding of it. He had left a message for Habersham when Jones had bought the contract to make sure it would be okay to at least observe the closing procedures, even if he wasn't needed for them.

"Hey, Joel, look, it's Roger Alcott. I know Mr. Jones is set to close with Valerie Browning next Monday, but if it'd be okay, I'd like to come by a little early just to see how you and your team actually do it. Can you call me back?"

As he hung up, he looked at the phone and laughed at himself.

Rog, let working men work and let the experts be experts.

He was pleasantly surprised when Joel called him back a few minutes later. Far from being offended, Habersham actually invited him to come in about 10:00 a.m., and he would give him a little tour of the process as it actually happened. As he hung up, he decided he'd take that morning off. Alliant could soldier on without him for a few hours.

Monday morning dawned cool and clear. Spring was still a few weeks off for Atlanta, but it wasn't really cold by Georgia standards. Nonetheless, Roger got up that morning and checked his Alliant email to find that Clayton Fredericks was asking to see him in his office at 10:00 a.m.

Damn! Of all the days. I'm working fifty-five hours a week and need to take a half day one day in a hundred, and it has to be today. Roger did some quick math in his head and realized that even if he wasn't needed to be present for the close (he had assigned the contract to Clive Jones, so Roger's proceeds were already in a drafted check in Joel's office)—and the close went off strictly as planned—and his meeting with Fredericks was only minutes and not the more likely hour—there was still no way he could make it from Alliant to Habersham's office by eleven. Gerber had told him plenty of times there would be questions at the closing table, and try as he might, he couldn't remember how long closing on his own house had taken. He had the vague impression of an hour, but he just couldn't be sure.

He decided to send Fredericks a response that he had a couple of personal things he had to handle that morning, but he would be happy to meet Clayton in his office by 1:00 p.m., if that was possible.

In his haste to respond to Fredericks' email, he forgot to hit send.

It was ironic that Roger's absence wasn't noticed until his team got there at 8:30 a.m. Two of his salesmen didn't miss a beat and merely assumed he was in the bathroom or a meeting. Roger not being in the office, to them at least, didn't mean Roger wasn't in the building, and despite the door being closed, they thought nothing of it and merely texted their boss to double check some items. The executive secretary who handled Roger's schedule and some of the administrative work Roger didn't have delegated elsewhere merely figured Roger had taken some personal time. Ultimately, no one on the team missed Roger because they all knew what they needed to be doing.

Roger responded to his team's texts and managed a few emails while he drank one last cup of coffee, then loaded his stuff in the Lexus and drove to Joel's office. When he arrived, he checked his phone, saw no pressing notifications, turned it to silent, then slipped it into his attaché case. Next, he went to find Habersham in his office. It was 9:51 a.m.

Joel greeted him warmly, offered him a cup of coffee, and then gave him the rundown of the closing procedure.

"Basically, Roger, a cash sale is the easiest close in the world. With clear title, a concise contract, and funds, you can buy just about anything in a half hour or so. You've already seen the contract you wrote, then there's the assignment fee, and there's the difference in the two. Your contract, which I know is the same as Mr. Gerber's, has that assignment placed as a fee between you and Mr. Jones. This is above and beyond the contract price you have with Mrs. Browning. You're getting paid, basically, a finder's fee for the house—the assignment fee, if you will—and even though Mr. Jones bought that contract from you for a larger amount than

Valerie Browning agreed to sell it to you for, you can't get paid on it until the house closes.

"Now, it's true some guys will simply cut a check to you when you assign them the contract, and that check is funded when the house closes. Other times, you'll have to come by the closing attorney's office or the office of the title company to pick up the check."

"And why is that?" asked Roger.

"Oh, let me count the ways. There could be a question of clear title, an absentee owner, you name it. Basically, if you assign a contract, you can plan on having the check in advance, although I wouldn't cash it until you're sure the house has closed.

"I've got guys I do this for that have never set foot in my office; we simply confirm the close has taken place. Sometimes, we mail the check to them or, in others, wire transfer it to their account. You can really do this thing a lot of different ways. But in the end, simply assigning the contract is the best way to save from paying me. If you were going to try to hide earnings or screw Mr. Jones, you might want to pull what we call a double close, but personally, I like single closes like what we're doing here."

Roger was slowly putting all his education together. "So, Joel, is there an advantage to doing a double close? I mean, there are two sets of docs, so twice as much in fees for you. Other than not being transparent, why do it at all?"

"Exactly, Roger. Your business is all about integrity and relationships. If you're assigning contracts, you already know you made some money, and your buyer already knows you made some money. Sometimes, though, you want to keep that money quiet. There's no easy answer, and in some places, you can't do it, and in others, you'd *better* do it."

Habersham laughed and went on to say, "But what do I know? I'm an attorney. Everyone knows I'm going to get paid. The truth is, the law reads differently in nearly every state, but some version of this is allowed in most of them. All the same, Roger, some folks like to keep their earnings quiet. For them, their privacy is more important than an extra grand or two in legal fees. That's especially true when you get into the bigger homes—guys flipping quarter million-dollar houses. That assignment fee can be fifty, seventy-five grand. Some guys can be resentful that a guy like you tracked down the deal and expects to get paid an annual salary for a week's worth of work."

"Joel, you know how hard it is to—"

Habersham put his hands up. "I'm not sayin' you didn't earn your money, Roger. Not at all. Remember, I get paid no matter how hard you worked. But some people—you gotta know your buyer. That's what I'm telling you."

Habersham checked his watch, excused himself for a moment, and three minutes later walked back into the room. "Roger, Mr. Jones and Miss Browning are here. Why don't you step into my office while we handle this close in the conference room?"

Tucked away in his attaché case, Roger's phone buzzed again, unheard. Before the lights went off, it showed four voicemails and seven missed calls. All were from Alliant and Clayton Fredericks.

* * * *

Fifteen miles from where Roger was effectively earning a paycheck and a diploma for his real estate education, Clayton Fredericks sat in his own office fuming. *That damned Alcott. Him and his big ideas. Him and his scheduling and hours and his plans and follow up and systems and nonsense!*

Fredericks was confident that only one of two things would keep Roger from coming to work and not having communicated with anyone—one, he was injured in an accident; two, he was at a job interview. The Alliant email system showed senders when emails were opened, so Clayton knew Roger had seen his email, and clearly, he didn't care enough to pick up the phone or even return the email, which was already open on his computer.

Angrily, Fredericks picked up the phone and tried Roger again. When the voicemail kicked on, Fredericks slammed his desk phone back onto the cradle.

The worst part of working with—or for—a man like Clayton Fredericks was that he wore his heart on his sleeve. Whether you were up or down the chain of command from him, you heard his thoughts—professional, personal, or otherwise. By 10:43 that morning, Fredericks' childish ranting had fueled the rumor mill at the Alliant water coolers.

Roger Alcott had told Fredericks to kiss off.

Roger had turned State's Evidence in the legal battle against Alliant.

Alcott was in a job interview.

* * * *

In reality, Roger was sitting in a comfortable chair in Joel Habersham's office in Roswell, Georgia, while a real estate deal he had nurtured and brought to life played out in the room beside him and cemented his belief that he could make a better living by taking responsibility for his own destiny.

Despite all his worry, the close proved to be almost anticlimactic. By 11:43, Valerie Browning had signed all her paperwork, and by 11:57, Clive Jones had executed his documents. Since it had been a cash sale, Habersham could distribute the checks, and the attorney handed Roger a check for $16,429. Clive Jones shook hands with Valerie Browning, stuck his head in the door to Habersham's office and thanked Roger again, and quickly left, but Roger lingered a moment. Joel stepped up beside Roger and asked simply, "How's it feel?"

Roger chuckled. "Pretty damn good, Joel," he said as he looked at the check in his hands. "Are they all this simple?"

Joel looked out the window. "Cash sales? Yeah, usually. Sometimes, the seller and the buyer are here at different times, but I think Mr. Jones likes to look folks in the eye when he buys a property. He's old money, you know. A remittance man from northern England who came here to get away from the cold. He's made, geez, I don't know *how* much money buying and selling, but his mother keeps sending him checks. He likes to do business the old-fashioned way, but you figure it out. This business is all about building bridges. Take care of folks, and they'll take care of you."

CHAPTER THIRTY-THREE

With that, Joel Habersham put out his hand, shook Roger's, and excused himself.

* * * *

Roger floated back to the Lexus and hit the Bluetooth to call Susan. He shared their good news and heard the tremble in Susan's voice and knew how happy she was. He also knew he'd pay hell for missing Fredericks' meeting, but at least he'd told the man he'd be late.

As he put the car in gear, he chanced to look down at the phone and saw eleven missed calls—all from Alliant and Clayton Fredericks. No big deal, probably just Fredericks being Fredericks. As Roger started to listen to the voicemails, though, his smile dimmed and then faded completely.

The first two messages sounded like the man was generally concerned. The next one, the voice had gotten terse. The fifth one would have made a sailor blush it was so filled with profanity and venom.

He tossed the phone in the seat next to him and decided that as pissed as Fredericks was, a few more minutes stewing shouldn't hurt, so he pulled into a convenience store to get a soda. Taking a long sip as he merged into traffic, he hit an unseen pothole and promptly spilled soda down the front of his white shirt and obligatory red tie.

Damn.

No worries, though. A lifetime of looking fresh and sharp no matter the time had taught Roger the importance of having an extra shirt and tie in the car, so he'd just have to swap out when he got to Alliant.

It wasn't the first time he'd changed shirts in a parking lot, and he bet it wasn't the last.

Fifteen minutes later as Roger was standing in a white t-shirt and unbuttoning a crisply starched shirt from the hanger in the back of the Lexus, his phone buzzed again.

It was Fredericks.

Roger looked at the check. It was well over a month's earnings from Alliant, and he'd done it in less than two weeks. He thought of the excitement in his wife's voice just minutes ago. His eyes glanced back to the phone and the clean shirt on a hanger in his hand.

Roger hung the shirt back on the hook in the back seat of his car and answered the phone.

Clayton seemed to come through the phone in a verbal assault. Where the hell had Roger been? Was he so damned important that he couldn't respond to emails? What was his problem? Roger closed up the car, locked the door, and began walking into the Alliant offices.

Still, the verbal lambasting continued. Roger finally gave up trying to get a word in edgewise and simply stood there, listening to what had essentially become a grown man having a temper tantrum. Alcott was pleasantly surprised the call didn't drop in the elevator, and as the doors opened up onto the fourth floor, he could suddenly hear the conversation in a weird sort of time delay. Maybe half a second from hearing Fredericks yelling from down the hall before he heard it on the phone. Clayton's secretary looked aghast as Roger walked in wearing his t-shirt, waved at the woman, and then winked.

Fredericks continued screaming into the phone, by now having moved from professional attacks to more personal ones as Roger opened the door. His brain couldn't seem to comprehend that the man he'd just been chastising on the phone now stood in front of him, and as quickly as the screaming had started, it stopped.

Standing there, red-faced and sweating, Clayton suddenly looked less like an angry man and more like a confused old man in the nursing home cafeteria.

Despite not having been asked, Roger sat down. He hadn't thought about what was about to come out of his mouth, he hadn't rehearsed it, and when he thought about it later, he realized it was truly a random decision. Roger put his fingers to his lips like a kindergarten teacher and shushed Fredericks.

"Clayton, I quit. You can have all of this—Alliant, the lawsuits, the teams, and the lies. You were never going to pay me the money you offered me, and you never gave a damn about what I wanted. You, the board, you're just using the rest of us to save your own asses. Alliant is going down, and you and the other rats are just trying to figure out how to float away gracefully."

Fredericks opened his mouth to say something, still in shock that he had seemingly conjured up Roger Alcott not in dress code. In some distant part of his brain, he realized that he'd never even seen the man's forearms. Roger shushed him again.

"I'm done. Your American dream isn't mine anymore. I'm going back to find out what it really means to live, to have a life, not to buy things that don't have any meaning. To create something of value and then to pass it along. Enjoy running what's left of this company into bankruptcy."

With that, he turned and walked out the still open door. The secretary had a look of amazement on her face, and in the short history of Alliant still to be written before the company did fail, Roger's last act as an executive did come to be a legend. It took Roger Alcott less than two minutes to get the things he needed out of his office—and only eight minutes after he left Clayton Fredericks, he sat in his car.

As he pulled out into traffic, Roger didn't look back or in the rearview mirror.

EPILOGUE—
FIFTEEN MONTHS LATER

*Start by doing what is necessary, then what is
possible, and suddenly you are doing the impossible.*

—St. Francis of Assisi

Roger Alcott sat on the back porch of his home on
the Monday morning that his sons' summer vacation began. He and Susan had settled into a routine
for effectively running Alcott Limited, and each day
inevitably started with breakfast as a family. Then,
after the boys were off to school, Roger and Susan sat
down and went over their goals for the day, the week,
and the month.

Now, with school out for the summer, he figured
Chris and Brent would be sleeping in late, and when
they finally got up, they'd probably ride their bikes
down to the pool or to a friend's house.

Personally, Roger didn't care, but he did relish the half hour or so of free time that Susan taking the boys to school allowed him. He did his affirmations, he journaled, and he usually scanned a news feed to keep abreast of current events.

Today, though, he found it ironic that the top local headline was the final nail in the bankruptcy proceedings and liquidation of Alliant Logistics Corporation the previous week. Clayton Fredericks had popped a golden parachute and never missed a paycheck. He had landed the same job he'd had before while the little people, who made the business actually run, had lost their jobs, their careers, and in some cases, their life savings as Alliant's stock price folded, along with their employee stock ownership disappearing. Personally, Roger had lost over $100,000 dollars in stock options, calculated against the price Alliant had traded at in its heyday.

But when was that? A lifetime ago. In the months since leaving, Roger and Susan had found a purpose and created a business that was producing a legacy. Today, with the arrival of a Federal Express van, that was going to change even more.

Four months ago, Roger and Susan had begun work on their first soft rehab. Ironically, the house had been built by Jim Arnold, the builder that Clive Jones had held in such high esteem. The major systems of the house had been well cared for—with a roof less than six years old and a heat pump that was, surprisingly, still under the factory warranty.

The Alcotts had been contacted by the children of the owner after the man had passed. The three kids, all in their forties, disliked one another and all lived far from Georgia. To them, the home they had grown up in and that their father had taken impeccable care of caused no fit of nostalgia, and Roger and Susan bought the house for $120,000 cash.

Throughout the Spring, the Alcotts' contractors had been busy with the house. The carpets were ripped out, the cabinets in the bathrooms and the kitchen were torn away, and what was once a cramped four-bedroom, two-bath became a spacious three-bedroom, two-and-a half-bathroom home with walk-in closets, a formal dining room, and a tidy, well-designed home office.

Susan had poured her heart into the work, using her ideas that she had used when decorating her home. She also used the sensible, bookkeeper's budget; she had spent just over thirty-six thousand dollars and then, last week, she and Roger had sold it. The price? $207,000.

Now seasoned veterans of real estate closings, the Alcotts had pre-signed the documents last week, the closing had been that Thursday, and the check, as they say, was in the mail.

Just then, Chris and Brent walked around the side of the house.

"Well, well, well, you boys are up early. I figured you two would sleep in to celebrate summer vacation."

"Yes, sir, well, good morning, Dad," said Brent. "We're going to make some money."

"Really? Well, it's a good morning for that. What makes you two suddenly decide to seek gainful employment?"

Chris rolled his eyes at the flowery language their dad was using. "Dad, we're fifteen. Next year, we can drive."

"That's right, son, *next* year."

"Well, we need money to buy a car, right? I mean, you're not giving up your Buick, and Mom definitely isn't going to let us have her Tahoe."

Brent looked to his brother for support and then said, "Well, we figured it would be good to start saving money now so that we can do like you guys did—pay cash for something. Fred Rosser—he's a junior at our school—well, his dad bought him a Camaro, and the payments are like $650 a month. That's waaaay too much. We want to get something a lot cheaper. Maybe a truck or something."

Chris nudged his brother. "*Two* trucks. You're too messy, and I don't want you to drive my car. You'll probably tear it up."

Roger nodded at his sons and smiled. "Well, now's the time. Get some money and find something you like. You can always spend the next year practicing driving it and fixing it up."

"Exactly!" said the boys in unison.

With that, Chris turned to go, and Brent looked at his dad, "How long will you and Mom be working today? We should be home by three or four. Can you text us if you need us before then?"

"Actually, son, you two need to be back here by about one."

"Daaaaaaad!" the boys said in unison.

"Trust me on this. I think you'll be happy to be here … and don't make any job plans before that."

The boys, somewhat perplexed, nonetheless agreed, and wandered off into the morning.

Federal Express was slow getting to the Alcotts' home that day, so it was actually 1:42 p.m. when the white van pulled into the driveway. The young man jumped out, and as he was reaching for the doorbell, Roger Alcott opened the door for him.

"Good afternoon! I'll bet I have to sign something?"

"Yes, sir, if you're Roger or Susan Alcott, you do."

Roger smiled. "No problem," he said as he scribbled his name on the electronic reader. He thanked the driver, closed the door, and turned to face his family. With a flourish, he opened the mailer and removed a check for $44,593—the proceeds of their sale after carrying the house for a few months, all the renovations, and the assorted fees. He smiled as he handed it to Susan.

"You did this. You're the one who pushed me to make these changes in my life ..." Roger paused. "... in *our* lives."

Susan looked at the check in her hands and started to cry. Brent and Chris, still confused, looked at each other and then their father for guidance. "Dang, what is it, Dad?"

"Show them, Susan."

The woman handed the check to her sons, who had a vague understanding of what their parents did but not of the money they made. The two young men's eyes grew wide as their minds calculated the size of the check in their hands.

"What is this for?"

Roger smiled. "It's for working hard and being clear on what it was we wanted. But more importantly, it's not about what it's for—it's about what it means."

Roger had run the numbers the day they signed the contract on the house. He knew, with all the Nieman properties cash-flowing the way they were and the

225

equity they now had in their portfolio, that he and Susan had finally reached Kiyosaki's Investor status.

"With this check, your mom and I will be taking off from work, most likely, for the summer. Remember this morning when I told you boys not to make any plans?"

The young men shook their heads, and in unison, said, "Yes, sir."

"Well, good. The reason being, we'll be taking the month off—starting tomorrow—for a family vacation. When I was kid, when a sports figure, like Michael Jordan or Joe Montana, had just won another championship, they'd be in commercials, and the announcer would ask, 'Now that you're a champion, what are you going to do?' And the answer they always gave was 'I'm going to Disney World.' So, we're going to take a week to go to Disney and then take the rest of the month and spend it at a house your mom and I rented on the beach in west Florida. Can you handle that?"

The boys were dumbfounded—and speechless.

Susan smiled. "Now might be a good time to say something, you two."

Chris didn't say anything, but Brent spoke up for the two of them. "Thank you!" And with that, the two young men rushed forward to embrace their parents.

* * * *

That evening, as the sun set on one of the best days that Roger Alcott could remember, he thought through the goals he had set for himself, his family, and his business. All the way back in January, he had begun the affirmation that he would close a deal worth $45,000 by June 1, and the fact that he was three days late and $407 short was hardly a reason to complain.

"Not quite what I wanted," he said to no one in particular, "but a whole lot better than I ever thought possible."

It had been nearly two years since this journey had begun, and every day, Roger woke up excited about the possibilities that greeted him and Susan in their business and their lives.

Alcott smiled, closed his journal, and walked inside to pack for their vacation.

ADDENDUM— ROGER'S NOTES

Start with the End in Mind:

* * * *

What I want:

- Passive income that allows me to work when I want and take off when I need or want to.

- I want to develop a business and investment strategy that I can leave to guarantee a legacy for my family.

- I want to be the master of my own destiny and to be able to build a company that serves a purpose—providing a solution, encouraging ownership, and one that means something.

- I want to learn to enjoy my career and make it a fun part of my life and involve my family.

- I want to be the guy smiling on his way to work.

* * * *

The *Four Entrepreneurial Freedoms* (trademarked by Dan Sullivan and Strategic Coach®, Inc.)

- Time

- Money

- Relationships

- Higher Purpose

What do The *Four Entrepreneurial Freedoms* mean to me?

Time? Time to spend being a father and a husband, not just a good provider. Time to spend on the hobbies I don't get to do, but I just own the stuff to do them—golf, hunting, being involved with the teams Brent and Chris play on. Time to spend with Susan, being a husband worthy of what she has put up with all these years that I chased a career to buy stuff.

Money? I want to lead and teach my family that money is a great thing, but spending money wisely is the smartest way to make more of it. Gerber said to view credit cards as investments, not consumable pieces. He also said that you're only truly free when you have enough passive income coming in each month to allow you not to work that day, or that week, or even that month. How the hell do I get there? I need to pay cash for the cars. I need to pay off the credit cards—or make sure that what I'm buying with them is deductible for the business *or* producing income far beyond what the interest is on the card.

I make $172,000 per year, so I need to replace that with passive income. If we struck out the debts on the cars and the credit cards, I could cut that number as low as $100,000 and still have the same quality of life for me and my family.

Relationships? I guess the relationships really are all about time and the ease at which you spend that time making money. If I can make money passively, then I have time to create and foster relationships. What's the relationship between time, money, and relationships? *Ask Gerber*—it's his idea!

I want to be a better father to my kids. No, I want to be a *dad*.

Higher Purpose? Maybe Higher Purpose really is just how you relate to the other three Freedoms. Maybe, until you can master the other three, you're out of luck on H.P.? That *feels* right, but it's like passive income; I'll have to work on it for a while to make it big enough to give me the success I want.

I want to set goals that aren't just based on business. They will be based on the things that matter to me—and those goals have to be based on these *Four Entrepreneurial Freedoms*.

* * * *

A cynic is a man who knows the price of everything, and the value of nothing.

—Oscar Wilde

Three Criticals

- **Deals**—Susan and I will use bandit signs (ask Gerber or Louis about where to buy them). From the callers, we can develop a list of buyers and sellers to work directly with. Louis said Craigslist sometimes works, but he doesn't like it.

- **Money**—Susan found some unused money we will put to work, but once we start wholesaling, we will use those profits to pay off Louis's portfolio and buy more wholesale properties.

- **People**—We're going to join the local meet up for real estate investors to continue to build our network. Porter Gale said your network is your net worth, and we've got to build that up quickly.

* * * *

Jack Canfield–author of *Chicken Soup for the Soul*

- Take responsibility!
- Events + Response = Outcomes

- An event plus your response will determine the outcome of anything

- youtube.com/watch?v=YeZoQwcTiSA

* * * *

Kiyosaki's Cash Flow Quadrant–by Robert Kiyosaki–author of *Rich Dad, Poor Dad*

- An investor is someone for whom the money works for them. It's truly passive income that means they can walk away from whatever they are doing for an indeterminate amount of time, and the money keeps working.

- Kiyosaki's Cash Flow Quadrant: youtu.be/xG3JzdkfHko

- Learn more: RichDad.com

* * * *

Sign ideas:

- 3Br/2ba. $59,000 cash
  Move-in ready
  Call 770-555-4821

- We buy houses!
  Any condition, any location
  Call 770-555-4821

- Home buyers wanted!
  Cash discounts, fast closing
  Call 770-555-4821

* * * *

Calculating the Offer Price:

65-70% of After-Repaired Value (ARV)
(ARV x discount percentage)-Repairs= Offer Price

Ex. 1—

- ARV= $100,000

- Repair Estimate= $15,000

- Offer is
  65%x$100,000=$65,000-$15,000=offer is
  $50K

Ex 2—

- ARV = $160,000

- Repair Estimate=$27,500

- Offer is 65%x$160,000=$104,000-$27,500. Offer is $76.5K

* * * *

You need to leave room for the various carrying costs of the property—taxes, attorney's fees, surveys, etc. Aim for 15-20% profit when you calculate

* * * *

Phone calls with sellers:

- Establish rapport—stay friendly, conversational, and non-confrontational. The call can never sound like an interrogation.

- Empathize with their challenges and motivations.

- Determine if the deal is all cash or if they are selling their equity.

- Set an appointment!

- Ask for their business—never say no for the other guy.

* * * *

Potential Buyer Investor Interview

Name:
Phone:
Email:
Company location:

Do you prefer move-in ready or rehab?
Do you have rehab teams in place?
What areas are you targeting?
How many properties did you buy last year?
How many properties do you plan to buy this year?
How come you don't plan to buy (Double the amount stated above)?

Bottleneck:
How do you finance?
What is your preferred home? Starter? Number of bedrooms/bathrooms? Square footage? One or two levels?

Demographics:
Do you base your purchase price on ARV?
How much equity do you expect to have per house?
What is your maximum purchase price?

Potential <u>Seller</u> Phone Interview

My name is _____

To whom am I speaking with? _____

Do you have a few minutes where I could ask you some questions about your property?

Great. Thank you.

1. Are you the owner of the property? Yes/ No

    a. (If answer is yes) How long have you owned the property?

2. What is the property address?

    a. # Bedrooms?

    b. # Bathrooms?

    c. Parking (IC/2C/1G/2G/3G/

    d. Approximate Sq. Ft.

    e. Approximately, how old is the house?

3. May I ask the reason you are selling the property?

4. How have you tried to sell your property so far?

5. How soon would you want to close the transaction?

6. What is your asking price?

7. How much do you think the home is worth all fixed up?

8. Is there anything still owed on the property?

    a. What is your mortgage balance?

    b. Mo. payment amount?

    c. Are your payments current? Yes / No

       i. If not, how far behind?

9. What repairs or upgrades would you say are still necessary to bring the home to retail condition?

NOTES:

Total Financial Awakening

AGREEMENT FOR PURCHASE & SALE FOR REAL ESTATE

AGREEMENT dated_____ between _____. Seller and **Your Company Name Here**. Buyer and/or assignees, whose address is Your Company Address Here.

1. **THE PROPETY**. The parties hereby agree that Seller will sell and Buyer will buy the following property, known by street address as _____ ("Property"). The sale price shall include the personal property [ ] Refrigerator [ ] Washer [_____ Dryer, except _____. Unless specifically excluded, all other personal property, fixtures and items will be included, whether or not affixed to the property or structures. **Seller represents and warrants** to the Buyer that the sewer line/ septic system is intact and in good working order. and that the Seller knows of no material structural defects in the Property. The **Property** is sold and purchased **"AS-IS"**.

2. **PURCHASE PRICE**. The total purchase price is $ _____ payable as follows: Earnest Money $_____ and Remaining Balance $_____ to be paid at time of closing.

3. **CLOSING**. Normal Seller's closing costs shall be paid by [ ] Buyer OR [ ] Seller, but Title Policy will be paid by Seller. Real property taxes and HOA dues and other usual items shall be prorated as of the date of Close of Escrow ("COE"). Closing will be held on or before _____. Seller to sign closing documents. Buyer and Seller agree to extend the closing deadline as necessary if the Seller cannot deliver clear title. Seller agrees to convey title by a **Warranty Deed**. Closing to take place at **Name of Title Company or Closing Attorney Here**, or the title company of Buyer's choice.

4. **POSSESSION**. Seller shall surrender possession of the property on or before the date of Closing. The property shall be delivered in broom-swept clean condition, free of all personal items and debris, and be of vacant status. The Buyer reserves the right to conduct a final "walk through" on or before the day of closing. Any remaining personal items left on or in the Property may be disposed of at Buyer's sole discretion and become property of Buyer at time of closing without exception.

5. **INSPECTION.** Buyer shall have access to the property for a period of 10 business days from date of acceptance for due diligence, inspections and feasibi study. Buyer's obligation to close escrow under this agreement is contingent upon the final inspection and approval of the Property by Buyer. This Agreement is subject to Management Approval for 10 days from date of acceptance.

6. **ACCESS.** Buyer shall be entitled to access property to show partners, lenders, inspectors and/or contractors prior to closing. Buyer may place an appropriate sign on the property prior to closing for prospective tenants, contractors and/or assigns.

7. **ATTORNEY'S FEES.** In the event an attorney is engaged by Buyer to enforce the terms of this Agreement or for the interpretation of any provision herei in dispute prior to COE, Seller agrees that the reasonable attorney's fees incurred in connection therewith will be credited to Buyer against the purchase price. If suit is brought to enforce the terms of this Agreement or to collect for the breach hereof, the prevailing party shall be entitled to recover, in addition to any other remedy, reasonable attorney's fees, court costs, costs of investigation and other related o comply incurred in connection therewi

8. **CURE PERIOD NOTICE.** Any perceived non- compliance with this Agreement shall be subject to a three day Cure Period Notice by the party claiming breach, which Notice shall describe the non-compliance in detail and by reference to the paragraph of this Agreement pertaining to the breach. If the non-compliance is not cured within three (3) calendar days after delivery of this notice ("Cure Period") the failure to comply shall become breach.

9. **OTHER PROVISIONS.** Seller acknowledges that Buyer is purchasing the Property in an attempt to make a profit. This Agreement is binding on Seller, Buy and their heirs, legal representatives, successors, and assigns. All representations and warranties in this Agreement shall survive closing. Seller authoriz Buyer to record a Memorandum of Agreement memorizing this Agreement with the appropriate county recorder. A copy of the Memorandum is attached. Seller has accepted this Agreement on Seller's own determination of the Property's value and has relied on any representation of Buyer regarding its value or marketability. Seller may employ licensed real estate agents, but said agents do not represent Seller. This Agreement sets forth th entire understanding of the parties with respect to the purchase of the Property. It may not be altered except by a writing dated and signed by both parties.

_____   _____   Phone: _____
Signer for Seller, Role: Date: Email: _____

_____   _____   Phone: _____
Signer for Seller, Role: Date: Email: _____

_____   _____
Authorized Signer for Buyer   Date

[ ] Addendum attached (initials required)   _____ _____ _____
                                               (Seller)   (Seller)   (Buyer)

ABOUT THE AUTHORS

Andrey Sokurec is a native of Belarus, formerly of the U.S.S.R. He obtained a degree in finance and banking at Belarus Economic University, where he won a full scholarship and graduated with honors. After college, he landed a position underwriting commercial loans for a large Belarus bank. He left that job to come to America, believing it to be the best place to realize his dreams.

By day, he worked as a manual laborer, and by night, he read books on business success. He purchased his first investment property in 2005. Andrey continued his education at Harvard Business School and has completed over $100 million in real estate transactions since then, building up a large portfolio of houses.

Andrey is a big believer in continuing education. He has learned firsthand from experts like Jack Canfield, author of *Chicken Soup for the Soul*, Robert Kiyosaki, author of *Rich Dad, Poor Dad*, and Harvey Mackay, author of *Swim with the Sharks*.

He has become a recognized authority in real estate as the founder of Midwest Real Estate Investment Association, as host of the TV Show "The Real Deal in Real Estate," and as a frequent guest presenter at investment summits and training seminars. He co-founded with his business partner, Alex Delendik, Homestead Road to integrate the entire process of buying homes, restoring them to marketability, and homesteading families. He lives with his wife and three children in Golden Valley, Minnesota.

Alex Delendik is a co-founder of Homestead Road where he oversees operations, including buying houses, restoring them, and homesteading new occupants. He is a native of Belarus, formerly of the U.S.S.R.

Aspiring to a career in international business, he studied engineering and economics, then worked in risk management for an Austrian bank. He came to the U.S. to expand his horizons, eventually leveraging his educational and banking background to partner with Andrey Sokurec in launching Homestead Road.

Connect with Andrey and Alex on You Tube at:
The Real Deal in Real Estate: youtube.com/channel/ UC3-vAtDHDGCbCot4Q3n07IQ?view_as= subscriber

Homestead Road:
youtube.com/HomesteadRoadMN

ABOUT HOMESTEAD ROAD

Homestead Road.

Feel the Joy®
OF SELLING YOUR HOUSE AS-IS.

Homestead Road® was founded in 2007 by business partners Andrey Sokurec and Alex Delendik with the vision of creating a different kind of home buying company. Since then, Homestead Road has helped well over 1,000 customers in Minnesota and Wisconsin sell their homes "as is," avoiding all the hassles and stress associated with selling a home.

Focused on providing every customer a "Feel the Joy" experience, Homestead Road has built a strong reputation for service that is reflected in excellent reviews on Google, Facebook, and BBB.org.

Homestead Road has been honored as a finalist for the BBB Torch Award for Ethics and has received numerous awards and recognition, including being featured on the *Inc. 5000* list of America's Fastest-Growing Privately Owned companies.

To learn more, visit HomesteadRoad.com.

Made in the USA
Coppell, TX
16 November 2020

41465586R00144